"I do not know whether you know all
that is to be known concerning small
mirrors : but of this, silence."

Arthur Machen, in a letter to
James Branch Cabell. 17 Feb. 1918

"Writers are liars."

Erasmus Fry, in conversation. 6 May 1986

The SANDMAN ™

DREAM COUNTRY
WRITTEN by NEIL GAIMAN

FEATURING CHARACTERS
CREATED by
NEIL GAIMAN, SAM KIETH & MIKE DRINGENBERG

THE SANDMAN: DREAM COUNTRY
Previously published in single magazine form as
THE SANDMAN 17-20. Copyright © 1990 DC Comics.
All rights reserved.

Cover and compilation copyright © 1991, 1995 DC Comics.
All rights reserved.

VERTIGO and all characters, their distinctive likenesses and
related elements featured in this publication are trademarks of
DC Comics. The stories, characters and incidents featured in this
publication are entirely fictional. DC Comics does not read or
accept unsolicited submissions of ideas, stories or artwork.

Cover and publication designed and
illustrated by Dave McKean.

Selected recoloring by Danny Vozzo.

DC Comics, 1700 Broadway, New York, NY 10019
A Warner Bros. Entertainment Company
Printed in Canada.

Hardcover ISBN: 1-56389-226-X
Third printing.

Softcover ISBN: 1-56389-016-X
Eleventh printing.

DREAM COUNTRY

INTRODUCTION
by STEVE ERICKSON

My father died last year. He'd been sick for some time. Two weeks after his death I had a dream about him. I was walking through the rooms of a very nice rest home; the windows were open, and outside the sky was and trees were swaying in the breeze. There was no one else in this home, no one but my father. He was sitting up in his bed and looked fine; he was tranquil and happy. He greeted me. Oh, I said, this is a dream.

This is not a dream, he answered.

We sat there for some time discussing this. On his lap he held a small plate and on the plate was a small pastry. He gave the pastry to me and said, Here, taste this; and I did. He said, You can taste it, can't you? and I could. He said, You can taste it because this isn't a dream. But I wouldn't believe him, and then I woke up. Except I didn't wake into consciousness but rather into *another* dream.

I've told a number of people about this since it happened, and every one of them has said the same thing. Every one of them has said that my father was right.

I'm writing this in the morning now. I'm writing this on the fine edge of that blade that's consciousness on one side and dream on the other, that thin silver horizon where you hover right before falling asleep, and right before completely waking. Neil Gaiman lives here all the damn time. He scribbles his stories and sends them out from the thin silver horizon whose bridge the rest of us traverse just twice a day. Gaiman is the troll who lives beneath the bridge; he exhales into word balloons the visions that flash only fleetingly across our gaze and then are gone with the next memory. Dreams of what we've loved and lost, dreams that are more vivid than our lives, dreams that tell you they aren't dreams, from which come the questions that trouble and enthrall and finally free our spirits, if we're brave enough for the answers. Gaiman's ideas, in other words, of a good time.

If I say that he writes circles around everyone else in comics, it's not simply to put him in a rare class with Gilbert Hernandez and Art Spiegelman and fellow Briton Alan Moore, but to speak literally: for Neil Gaiman's stories in *The Sandman* descend concentrically through a narrative maze to a room at the center, where you expect to find a confessional and instead step into a veldt that stretches as far as the eye can see.

In the same fashion the character called Dream or Morpheus or Sandman lurks at the center of every story in this collection by inhabiting the outer passages. In "Calliope," a once successful novelist who's become so impotent in his art he can no longer write makes a bargain to enslave his muse, devouring her for his inspiration when he isn't ravaging her for his pleasure. In "A Dream of a Thousand Cats" a pilgrimage of cats, their world dominated by people who snatch their kittens, stuff them in bags and hurl them to oblivion, find they can transform their destiny through a memory dreamt in common. "A Midsummer-Night's Dream" follows a wandering sixteenth-century theatrical troupe into a performance where everything will change mid-play; when the masks are lifted at the end, the actors revealed aren't the same as the ones who put the masks on. And an old comic book character, unnamed here to those of us who don't ordinarily spend a lot of time in comicbookland, runs out of masks of her own in "Façade." She can transform every element of her existence but the one that matters, because the equation of the soul is written in a physics both far simpler and more complicated than any that men have devised. Only the foxiest little incarnation of Death you ever saw can comfort her desolation; in the final blast of sunlight, when the thin silver horizon bathes her in its furious glory, Element Girl is delivered from her mortal chemistry to something that defies decomposition. Then the eternal face of the heart gazes with pity on the ravaged face of the psyche.

Dream Country follows the previous Sandman novel, *The Doll's House*, published last year. I'd say that *The Doll's House* is Gaiman's masterpiece because at the time he wrote it, it was; but then he went and complicated matters by writing *A Season of Mists* in *Sandman* issues #21-28, which was better, confronting the Dreambearer with the necessity of his own redemption. In some ways, however, it may be *Dream Country*, the interlude between these two novels, that best defines what *Sandman* has been about. As rendered by the splendid art of Kelley Jones, Charles Vess, Colleen Doran, and Malcolm Jones, it holds the dark mirror of Gaiman's efforts up to the variety of cracked lives listed above, any one of which we're bound to bear some resemblance to. This, then, is the Sandman of your particular bridge, the bridge you came across this morning, the one you will return across tonight. Don't pay too much attention to the troll underneath, cheeky bastard that he

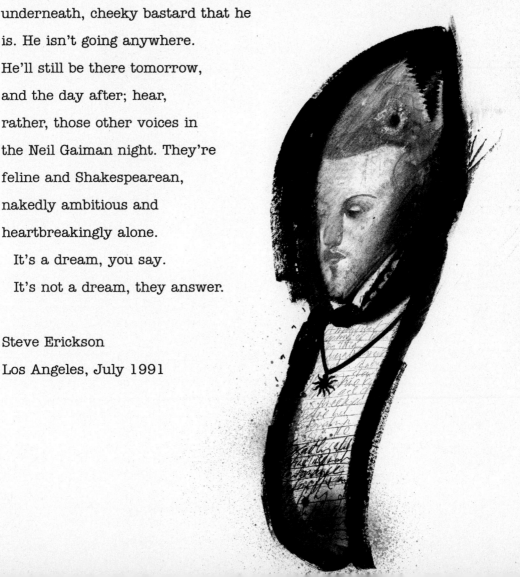

is. He isn't going anywhere.

He'll still be there tomorrow,

and the day after; hear,

rather, those other voices in

the Neil Gaiman night. They're

feline and Shakespearean,

nakedly ambitious and

heartbreakingly alone.

    It's a dream, you say.

    It's not a dream, they answer.

Steve Erickson

Los Angeles, July 1991

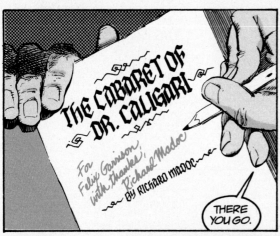

THE CABARET OF DR. CALIGARI

For Felix Garrison, with thanks, Richard Madoc

BY RICHARD MADOC

THERE YOU GO.

THIS IS *GREAT*. IT'S A REAL *THRILL* FOR ME, TO, YOU KNOW, BE ABLE TO DO SOMETHING FOR ONE OF MY HEROES. I *LOVED* THE BOOK. *AMAZING* STUFF.

SO, UM, WHAT DO YOU NEED THE BEZOAR FOR?

LIKE YOU WERE ASKING THE OTHER DAY-- WHERE DO WRITERS GET OUR CRAZY IDEAS? HEH.

IT'S RESEARCH, REALLY.

I HEARD YOU WERE WRITING A SEQUEL TO *THE CABARET*-- I'M REALLY EXCITED.

OH. GREAT.

UH, THAT'S THE PHONE. LISTEN, THANKS AGAIN FOR THE THING.

NO PROBLEM. I KNOW HOW *BUSY* YOU ARE. I'LL JUST LET MYSELF OUT, THEN. 'BYE.

BREEP BREEP

HELLO? RICHARD MADOC SPEAKING.

OH. HI, HARRY.

RICK? IT'S HARRY. LISTEN, WE HAVE TO *TALK*. YOUR PUBLISHERS WERE ONTO ME AGAIN TODAY.

LISTEN, THE NOVEL'S ALMOST NINE MONTHS OVERDUE, AND THEY'RE THREATENING TO CAUSE TROUBLE. YOU'RE IN BREACH OF CONTRACT, RICK. IS IT FINISHED *YET*?

NEARLY FINISHED.

WELL, *HOW* MUCH HAVE YOU GOT TO GO?

IT'S *ALMOST* FINISHED, HARRY. YOU CAN'T RUSH THESE THINGS. ANOTHER COUPLE OF WEEKS, MAYBE, OKAY?

LISTEN, I'M *REALLY* BUSY. I'LL GET BACK TO YOU. OKAY?

2

HOW MUCH OF THE NOVEL HAVE I WRITTEN? HONESTLY?

NOTHING.

NOT A *WORD*.

WHO IS IT?

RICHARD MADOC, TO SEE ERASMUS FRY.

I'LL BE STRAIGHT DOWN.

ARE YOU ALONE?

YES. IT'S JUST ME. I'VE GOT IT.

WELL, COME *IN*, DEAR BOY. COME *IN*.

I'M *NOT* SORRY THAT I'M NOT DRESSED FOR VISITORS. WHEN YOU GET TO MY AGE, YOU DON'T GIVE A TOSS WHAT YOU LOOK LIKE. HEH.

DON'T JUST *STAND* THERE. COME IN.

③

HOW ARE YOU, M'BOY? WRITTEN ANYTHING PROFOUND AND STIRRING RECENTLY?

AH-- AN EXCUSE FOR A SHERRY.

LET ME TELL YOU ABOUT BEZOARS. WORD COMES FROM THE PERSIAN. *PAD-ZAHR*. IT MEANS COUNTER-POISON. ANTIDOTE. MAINLY FOUND IN THE STOMACHS OF GOATS AND GAZELLES.

YOU *KNOW* I HAVEN'T, MR. FRY.

NO. WE'LL GO INTO MY STUDY, AND YOU CAN SHOW ME MY PRESENT.

CHEAP STUFF, OF COURSE. I'M NOT WASTING THE *GOOD* STUFF ON A LITTLE *SHIT* LIKE YOU.

ONCE BELIEVED TO POSSESS MYSTIC POWERS : THEY CAN REMEDY POISON, MAKE THE SICK WELL. EDWARD IV SURVIVED THE EFFECTS OF A POISONED WOUND, DUE SOLELY TO A BEZOAR IN HIS POSSESSION.

QUEEN ELIZABETH THE FIRST HAD A BEZOAR SET IN GOLD, WITH UNICORN'S HORN, GIVEN TO HER BY JOHN DEE, HER SPY AND MAGICIAN.

FOR THE COMMON PEOPLE, APOTHECARIES WOULD LEND OUT BEZOARS AT EXTORTION-ATE RATES, FOR A WEEK, OR A FORTNIGHT...

WILL YOU *SHUT UP?* I HAVEN'T WRITTEN A *WORD* IN A *YEAR*--*NOTHING* I HAVEN'T THROWN AWAY! DO YOU *KNOW* WHAT THAT'S *LIKE?*

WHEN IT'S *JUST* YOU, AND A BLANK SHEET OF PAPER?

WHEN YOU CAN'T THINK OF A *SINGLE* THING WORTH SAYING, A SINGLE *CHARACTER* THAT PEOPLE COULD *BELIEVE* IN, A SINGLE *STORY* THAT HASN'T BEEN TOLD A *THOUSAND* TIMES BEFORE...

4

OH YES. RAPUNZEL, LET DOWN YOUR HAIRBALL. A GENUINE TRICHINO-BEZOAR. THE SMELL COMES FROM THE PARTLY DIGESTED PARTICLES OF FOOD, TRAPPED IN--

I'M SORRY. I'M LECTURING AGAIN. AN OLD WRITER WITH NO ONE TO TALK TO GETS FOND OF THE SOUND OF HIS OWN VOICE...

OF COURSE I KNOW WHAT IT'S LIKE. DON'T BE A FOOL, BOY.

LET ME SEE MY PRESENT.

I WILL PUT THE BEZOAR WITH THE REST OF THEM. I SUPPOSE THAT YOU WANT HER NOW.

DID YOU BRING ANY CLOTHES?

CLOTHES? I DIDN'T KNOW I...

NEVER MIND. I HAVE AN OLD COAT YOU MAY USE.

I CAUGHT HER ON MOUNT HELICON, YOU KNOW. 1927. GREECE. I WAS 27. I'LL BE 87 NEXT YEAR.

THE HARDEST PART WAS GETTING HER BACK TO ENGLAND.

THEY SAY ONE OUGHT TO WOO HER KIND, BUT I MUST SAY I FOUND FORCE MOST EFFICACIOUS...

AFTER ALL, I GOT THE FAME AND THE GLORY. I CREATED THE NOVELS, THE POEMS, THE PLAYS...

I DON'T NEED HER ANY MORE, MADOC. AND YOU DO.

HERE SHE IS.

SHE WAS BATHING IN A SPRING, AND I CAUGHT HER AND BOUND HER WITH MOLY--SORCERER'S GARLIC, AS IT'S SOMETIMES CALLED--AND WITH CERTAIN RITUALS.

15

5

RICHARD, *THIS* IS *CALLIOPE*. THE YOUNGEST OF THE NINE MUSES. SHE WAS *HOMER'S* MUSE, SO SHE *OUGHT* TO BE GOOD ENOUGH FOR YOU.

DON'T GET YOURSELF ALL WORKED UP, CALLIOPE.

NO, *THIS* IS RICHARD MADOC. HE'S A NOVELIST--OR AT LEAST, HE'S WRITTEN ONE *EXTREMELY* SUCCESSFUL FIRST NOVEL, AND HAS FOUND HIMSELF QUITE UNABLE TO WRITE ANYTHING ELSE.

WHAT WOULD YOU WITH ME NOW, ERASMUS? AM I NOW TO PERFORM FOR YOUR AMUSEMENT? IS THIS MAN TO BE OUR AUDIENCE?

CALLIOPE, I'M GIVING YOU TO RICHARD. YOU'RE *HIS* NOW.

BUT YOU SAID--YOU TOLD ME, YOU *PROMISED* THAT YOU WOULD *FREE* ME BEFORE YOU DIED. YOU SAID I COULD HAVE MY FREEDOM...

PUT NOT YOUR TRUST IN *PRINCES*, MY DEAR.

NOR IN AN AGING AUTHOR WHO HAS NEVER BEEN WHAT ONE MIGHT CALL A *SHINING* EXAMPLE WHEN IT CAME TO KEEPING HIS *WORD*...

WRITERS ARE *LIARS*, MY DEAR. SURELY YOU HAVE REALIZED THAT BY *NOW*?

TAKE THE LITTLE COW *AWAY*, MADOC. I NEVER WANT TO SEE *EITHER* OF YOU AGAIN.

HOWEVER, IF YOU EVER HAPPEN TO FEEL A SPARK OF GRATITUDE, YOU MIGHT WANT TO PERSUADE SOME PUBLISHER TO BRING *"HERE COMES A CANDLE"* BACK INTO PRINT.

I WAS *PARTICULARLY* PROUD OF THAT ONE.

7

AND MADOC TOOK CALLIOPE BACK TO HIS HOME, AND LOCKED HER IN THE TOPMOST ROOM, WHICH HE HAD PREPARED FOR HER.

HIS FIRST ACTION WAS TO RAPE HER, NERVOUSLY, ON THE MUSTY OLD CAMP BED.

SHE'S NOT EVEN HUMAN, HE TOLD HIMSELF. *SHE'S THOUSANDS OF YEARS OLD.* BUT HER FLESH WAS WARM, AND HER BREATH WAS SWEET, AND SHE CHOKED BACK TEARS LIKE A CHILD WHENEVER HE HURT HER.

IT OCCURRED TO HIM MOMENTARILY THAT THE OLD MAN MIGHT HAVE CHEATED HIM: GIVEN HIM A REAL GIRL. THAT HE, RICK MADOC, MIGHT POSSIBLY HAVE DONE SOMETHING WRONG, EVEN CRIMINAL...

BUT AFTERWARDS, RELAXING IN HIS STUDY, SOMETHING SHIFTED INSIDE HIS HEAD.

HE HAD BEEN WRITING FOR THREE HOURS BEFORE HE SURFACED ENOUGH TO REALIZE THAT HE HAD BEGUN HIS SECOND NOVEL.

HE SWITCHED ON THE WORD PROCESSOR TO WRITE IT DOWN BEFORE IT FLED.

CHAPTER THREE.
"AND SOME IN VELVET GOWNS"

"Your face," he said to her. "What have you done to your face?"

Marion shrugged. "I wanted to look on the outside like I do on the inside," she said simply, not putting down the knife.

8

GRACIOUS LADIES, MOTHER OF THE CAMENAE, HEAR MY PRAYER.

MELETE, MNEME, AIODE, ATTEND MY SUPPLICATION.

IT IS I, YOUR DAUGHTER CALLIOPE, WHO CALLS YOU, AS I HAVE CALLED YOU A THOUSAND TIMES. I...

I IMPLORE YOU, LADIES, DELIVER ME FROM THIS PLACE AND THIS TIME.

TO WHOM CAN I SPEAK, IN MY GRIEF? I WHO AM LADEN WITH WRETCHEDNESS. LADIES OF MEDITATION, REMEMBRANCE AND SONG...

...HEARKEN TO ME.

ALL RIGHT. ENOUGH, BEAUTIFUL VOICE. WHY DO YOU CALL US?

WE FEEL YOUR PAIN, DAUGHTER, BUT WE CANNOT HELP YOU.

YOU WERE SNARED UPON HELICON ACCORDING TO THE MYSTERIES. YOU ARE LAWFULLY BOUND.

BUT IT IS NOT JUST, MY MOTHERS. I CAN BEAR THIS BURDEN NO MORE.

IS THERE NOTHING YOU CAN DO? NO ONE WHO CAN INTERCEDE ON MY BEHALF?

THERE ARE FEW OF THE OLD POWERS WILLING OR ABLE TO MEDDLE IN MORTAL AFFAIRS IN THESE DAYS, CALLIOPE.

HEHH. ONLY THE ENDLESS WILL NEVER DIE--AND EVEN THEY ARE HAVING A DIFFICULT TIME OF LATE.

MANY GODS HAVE DIED, MY DAUGHTER; WHILE ASPECTS OF OTHER GODS HAVE BEEN LOST FOREVER.

STILL, EVERY LITTLE BIT HELPS, AS THE OLD WOMAN SAID WHEN SHE PISSED IN THE SEA.

9

THE ENDLESS-- NOW, THERE'S A THOUGHT. AFTER ALL, THE DREAM-KING AND CALLIOPE WERE CLOSE, LONG AGO. FOR A SHORT WHILE. WEREN'T YOU, MY PET?

NOT FOR LONG. AND REMEMBER, SISTER-SELF, THEY DID NOT PART ON THE BEST OF TERMS.

BUT SHE DID BEAR HIS CUB.

THAT BOY-CHILD WHO WENT TO HADES FOR HIS LADY-LOVE, AND DIED IN THRACE, TORN APART BY THE SISTERS OF THE FRENZY, FOR HIS SACRILEGE.

NOT HIM. NOT AFTER WHAT HE DID TO ME. HE HATES ME FOR THAT, AND I DESPISE HIM. I WOULD NOT ACCEPT HIS HELP.

FOOLISH CHILD. ONEIROS IS IN NO POSITION TO HELP YOU, EVEN IF HE WISHED TO-- WHICH IS UNLIKELY, TO PUT IT MILDLY.

YOU SEE, JUST LIKE YOU, CALLIOPE, YOUR ONE-TIME ADMIRER HAS BEEN ENSNARED BY MORTALS.

AND WHILE YOU ARE IMPRISONED IN YOUR TOWER, HE IS IMMURED BENEATH THE GROUND.

I AM SORRY, MY LITTLE ONE. YOUR PRAYERS WERE WASTED. THERE IS NOTHING WE CAN DO FOR YOU, AND NOTHING YOU CAN DO BUT HOPE.

NO--PLEASE, COME BACK, PLEASE. THERE MUST BE SOMETHING, THERE MUST BE SOMEONE WHO CAN FREE ME...

PLEASE... SEND SOMEONE... ANYONE...

EVEN ONEIROS.

IT HAD BEEN HER OWN FAULT.

SPRING, 1927. MOUNT HELICON.

SHE HAD ONLY RETURNED FOR A BRIEF TIME, LURED PERHAPS BY NOSTALGIA...

SHE HAD LAID DOWN HER SCROLL, AND WAS BATHING IN A CLEAR POOL, REMEMBERING THE LOST, GOLDEN DAYS: WHEN THE NINE WERE STILL SOUGHT AND WOOED AND NEEDED...

WHEN THE MUSIC OF THE SPHERES STILL ECHOED IN MORTAL SOULS.

IN ONE HAND HE HELD MOLY FLOWERS, THAT HAD POWER OVER HER KIND, AND IN HIS OTHER HAND HELD HER SCROLL.

WHICH ONE ARE YOU? HE HAD ASKED HER.

CALLIOPE, SHE TOLD HIM.

KALL-I-OH-PEE, HE HAD ECHOED, AS IF HE WERE TASTING HER NAME.

AND THEN HE SMILED. WELL, HE SAID, YOU CAN CALL ME MASTER.

AND THEN HE BURNED HER SCROLL.

HEY! GREAT NEWS! I'VE FINISHED THE NOVEL. IT'S CALLED *"MY LOVE SHE GAVE ME LIGHT."* TWO DRAFTS IN FIVE WEEKS. AND IT'S ALL GOOD STUFF.

I AM PLEASED FOR YOU. NOW WILL YOU LET ME GO?

ARE YOU *OUT* OF YOUR *MIND?* THIS IS JUST THE BEGINNING. COME HERE, GORGEOUS. LET'S MAKE TWO AND A HALF MINUTES OF SQUELCHING NOISES.

PLEASE, MADOC. LET ME GO. STOP FORCING ME TO DO THESE THINGS.

LISTEN. YOU'RE MY POSSESSION, UNTIL I TELL YOU THAT YOU'RE FREE. DON'T FORGET IT.

YOU'RE MY *PERSONAL* MUSE, SWEETHEART. NOW.

LET'S PARTY.

⑪

FEBRUARY, 1989.

THANK YOU, ALL OF YOU, *SO* MUCH. YOU KNOW, WHEN I FIRST TOLD MY AGENT I WAS PLANNING TO WRITE A PLAY, HE SAID RIC, YOU'RE CRAZY.

SO I GOT A NEW AGENT. *HA HA HA.*

APRIL, 1989.

...WE'VE BEEN ACTIVELY DISCUSSING YOUR ORIGINAL OFFER TO WRITE A SCREENPLAY, IF WE LET YOU DIRECT. I'M PLEASED TO TELL YOU THAT--

HARVEY, IT'S TOO LATE. I'VE ALREADY SIGNED A THREE-FILM DEAL IN THE U.S. BUT *THANKS*, Y'KNOW.

MAY, 1989.

RIC MADOC BUYS A NEW HOUSE, IN CHELSEA. HE'S BUSY ON PRE-PRODUCTION FOR THE FILM, AND MOST OF THE MOVING IS DONE FOR HIM.

HE MOVES HIS MOST VALUABLE POSSESSION HIMSELF, THOUGH, LATE ONE SPRING NIGHT.

SEPTEMBER, 1989.

NO. NO, I LIKE HOLLYWOOD WELL ENOUGH, BUT I'M REALLY PLEASED TO BE GOING HOME. TWO MONTHS AWAY IS ENOUGH FOR ME.

HI! IN CASE YOU'VE JUST TUNED IN, I'M TALKING TO RIC MADOC, WRITER, POET AND SOON-TO-BE FILM DIRECTOR, ABOUT HIS NEW EPIC NOVEL, *"EAGLE STONES"!*

OCTOBER, 1989.

TRAILERS

...WRITER OF THE BEST-SELLING NOVEL, *"EAGLE STONES,"* TALKED TO US ABOUT HIS EXTRA-ORDINARY NEW FILM, *"...AND THE MADNESS OF CROWDS,"* AND WE'LL BE SHOWING SOME EX*CLUS*IVE FOOTAGE.

THAT'S *ALL*...AFTER THIS SHORT BREAK.

MARCH, 1990

RIC MADOC'S *"...AND THE MADNESS OF CROWDS"*

NOMINATED FOR 3 OSCARS, BEST ORIGINAL SCREENPLAY, BEST DIRECTOR, BEST PICTURE

13

OH. IT'S YOU.

THEY... THEY *TOLD* ME THAT YOU HAD BEEN IMPRISONED. JUST LIKE ME.

They spoke the truth. I was imprisoned. But, as you can see, I am free now.

THEN *PLEASE* -- BY THE LOVE I ONCE HAD FOR YOU. BY -- WHATEVER YOU FELT FOR ME. PLEASE.

MAKE HIM GIVE ME MY FREEDOM. MAKE HIM LET ME *GO.*

the booknook

BBC

ALTHOUGH YOU'VE BEEN COMPARED TO THE MULTI-TALENTED JEAN COCTEAU, AND TO A LESSER EXTENT TO WRITER-DIRECTORS LIKE CLIVE BARKER...

...IT SEEMS TO ME THAT THE CREATOR WHO PERHAPS YOU MOST RESEMBLE IS THE LATE 1940'S CULT FIGURE, ERASMUS FRY...

EXCUSE ME -- YOU SAID *"THE LATE."* HE'S DEAD?

LAST SUMMER. DID YOU KNOW HIM?

I DIDN'T *KNOW* HIM. WE *MET*...ON A COUPLE OF OCCASIONS. HE WAS... *INTERESTED* IN MY WORK.

AH. ANYWAY, LIKE YOU, FRY WAS ABOVE ALL A CREATOR OF EPICS, OF HUGE, TOWERING ROMANCES...

24

14

...WENT VERY WELL, I THOUGHT. IT'LL BE BROADCAST IN JUNE-- WE'LL LET YOU KNOW THE EXACT DATE.

THANKS. I SUPPOSE FRY MUST HAVE DIED WHILE I WAS SHOOTING IN THE *U.S.* OLD AGE, I SUPPOSE. HE *MUST'VE* BEEN ALMOST NINETY.

OH NO. HE *POISONED* HIMSELF.

IT'S QUITE FUNNY. APPARENTLY THE LAST THING HE DID WAS WRITE A LETTER TO HIS OLD PUBLISHERS, *BEGGING* THEM TO BRING ONE OF HIS BOOKS BACK INTO PRINT...

"HERE COMES THE CANDLE," I SUPPOSE.

IT WAS A GOOD BOOK. PERHAPS MY *FAVORITE* BOOK, WHEN I WAS GROWING UP. VERY MOVING, AND HONEST, AND STRANGE.

POOR OLD SOD.

I THINK THAT WAS IT. HOW DID YOU GUESS?

15

CHRIST! WHAT ARE YOU DOING IN MY HOUSE? WHO LET YOU IN?

I DON'T KNOW WHO YOU ARE, BUT I WANT YOU OUT OF HERE, **NOW**, OR I'M CALLING THE POLICE.

Nobody let me in, Richard Madoc.

Be quiet.

You are keeping a woman imprisoned here, Richard Madoc. Keeping her against her will.

I have come to request that you set her free.

16

ARE YOU OUT OF YOUR *MIND*? THERE'S *NO* WOMAN *HERE*. NOW GET *OUT* OF HERE! DO YOU KNOW WHO I *AM*? THERE--THERE'S *A LAW* AGAINST PEOPLE LIKE YOU!

ARE YOU GOING TO CALL THE POLICE? IS *THAT* IT?

No. I will not call any human agency.

Just let her go.

BUT YOU DON'T UNDERSTAND-- I *NEED* HER. IF I DIDN'T HAVE HER, I WOULDN'T BE ABLE TO *WRITE*. I WOULDN'T HAVE *IDEAS*.

I CAN'T FREE HER *YET*. NOT *NOW*. MAYBE IN A YEAR OR SO.

LOOK, I HAVE MONEY--AN AWFUL LOT OF MONEY-- AND...

Hold your tongue.

She has been held captive for more than sixty years. Stripped of all possessions. Demeaned, abused, and hurt.

I... know how she must feel.

And you will not free her because "You need the ideas?"

You disgust me, Richard Madoc.

You want ideas? You want dreams? You want stories?

Then ideas you will have. IDEAS IN ABUNDANCE.

17

UHHHNN.

I JUST HAD THIS WEIRD DREAM...WHAT DO YOU *KNOW* ABOUT IT? *HUH?* ARE *YOU* DOING THAT? GIVING ME NIGHTMARES?

ARE YOU *DOING* IT?

TELL ME!

TELL ME, OR SO HELP ME, I'LL, I'LL....

NO, I AM NOT DOING IT, RICHARD MADOC.

YOU HAVE MET *ONEIROS,* WHOM THE ROMANS CALLED THE SHAPER OF FORM.

HE WAS ONCE MY LOVER, AND HE WAS THE FATHER OF MY SON.

I DIDN'T KNOW YOU'D EVER HAD A SON.

YOU KNOW NOTHING ABOUT ME, RICHARD MADOC.

I AM REAL, RICHARD. I AM MORE THAN A RECEPTACLE FOR YOUR SEED, OR AN INSPIRATION FOR YOUR TALES.

STILL, IT IS TOO LATE NOW TO LET THAT CONCERN YOU.

GOODBYE, RICHARD MADOC. ENJOY YOUR PARTY.

18

A *TIME OUT*, PLEASE. AND A *STANDARD*.

RIGHT-HO. SAW YOU ON THE TELLY THE OTHER NIGHT. I SAID TO MY WIFE, HE BUYS PAPERS FROM ME. SHE SAID, HE NEVER, I SAID, HE DOES. ONE TWENTY, PLEASE.

AH... I'M GOING TO A PARTY...

YOU KNOW, I COULD WRITE A WHOLE STORY SET AT A PARTY. POSSIBLY SOMETHING COULD HAVE HAPPENED TO THE WORLD OUTSIDE -- A HOLOCAUST OF SOME KIND...

THESE PEOPLE ARE PARTYING AGAINST THE DARKNESS.

HERE! MISTER MADOC! THAT'S ONE POUND TWENTY YOU OWE ME!

THE FRATERNITY OF CRITICS. IN REALITY A DARK BRETHREN, LINKED BY PROFANE RITES AND BLOOD VOWS. TO DESTROY AN AUTHOR THEY SACRIFICE A CHILD AND PERFORM A CRITICAL MASS...

A CITY IN WHICH THE STREETS ARE PAVED WITH TIME.

A TRAIN FULL OF SILENT WOMEN, PLOWING FOREVER THROUGH THE TWILIGHT.

HEADS MADE OF LIGHT. A SMALL PIECE OF BLUE CARDBOARD. A PLUM, SWEET AND TART AND COLD. A WERE-GOLDFISH WHO TRANSFORMS INTO A WOLF AT FULL MOON.

TWO OLD WOMEN TAKING A WEASEL ON HOLIDAY.

GRYPHONS SHOULDN'T MARRY. VAMPIRES DON'T DANCE.

A MAN WHO INHERITS A LIBRARY CARD TO THE LIBRARY IN ALEXANDRIA.

A ROSE BUSH, A NIGHTINGALE, AND A BLACK RUBBER DOG-COLLAR.

19

A MAN WHO FALLS IN LOVE WITH A PAPER DOLL.

THE SUN SETTING OVER THE PARTHENON. SHARK'S TEETH SOUP.

IS SOMETHING WRONG? I'M A DOCTOR. STAND BACK, PLEASE.

GOOD GRIEF--RICHARD MADOC!

WHAT'S THE MATTER, OLD FELLOW?

I'M JUST HAVING IDEAS. SO MANY...

AN OLD MAN IN SUNDERLAND WHO OWNED THE UNIVERSE, AND WHO KEPT IT IN A JAM-JAR IN THE DUSTY CUPBOARD UNDER HIS STAIRS,...

MY HOME IS JUST AROUND THE CORNER. LEAN ON ME. DO YOU REMEMBER ME--FELIX GARRISON?

IT'S THE IDEAS. WHERE WE GET THEM FROM. A SESTINA ABOUT SILENCE, USING THE KEY WORDS DARK, RAGGED, NEVER, SCREAMING, FIRE, KISS.

FELIX GARRISON F.R.C.S.

COME ON INSIDE. YOU'LL HAVE TO TELL ME WHAT'S THE MATTER. SOON HAVE YOU FEELING BETTER.

GOD--WHAT DID YOU DO TO YOUR HANDS?

A BIOGRAPHY OF KEATS, FROM THE LAMIA'S VIEWPOINT...

ALL THE PICTURES IN MY HEAD. I HAD TO GET THEM DOWN, BUT I DIDN'T HAVE ANY PAPER, OR INK. SO I USED THE WALL.

AND MY FINGERTIPS.

20

LL THE IDEAS, INSIDE. ALL THE CTURES AND POEMS AND TALES ND SONGS AND PLAYS AND SPEECHES AND FRAGMENTS... THEY'RE ALL COMING OUT. YOU MUST HELP ME.

I'LL GIVE YOU A SEDATIVE, AND BANDAGE THOSE FINGERS.

NO! NO... I'M SORRY. NOTHING LIKE THAT.

IT'S HER REVENGE, YOU SEE. OR HIS REVENGE. I SAID I NEEDED THE IDEAS-- BUT THEY'RE COMING SO FAST, SWAMPING ME, OVER-WHELMING ME...

YOU HAVE TO MAKE THEM STOP.

HERE-- THIS WILL CALM YOUR NERVES.

NO! I TOLD YOU.

LOOK-- GO TO MY HOUSE. THE KEYS ARE IN MY POCKET IF-- IF YOU CAN TAKE THEM OUT FOR ME. I DON'T THINK I CAN USE MY HANDS ANYMORE.

GO UPSTAIRS. AT THE TOP OF THE HOUSE THERE'S A ROOM. THERE'S A WOMAN IN THERE.

LET HER OUT. SHE'S LOCKED UP IN THERE, YOU SEE.

TELL HER-- TELL HER SHE CAN GO. THAT I FREE HER. MAKE HER LEAVE. MAKE HER GO AWAY.

I SIGNED A BOOK FOR YOU ONCE, DIDN'T I?

OH GOD. PLEASE.

ALL RIGHT. STAY HERE. I'LL BE BACK SOON.

MAKE IT STOP. TELL HER I'M SORRY.

MAGICAL AND ALCHEMICAL TRADITIONS SEEN AS A CARGO CULT; AUREOLUS THEOPHRASTUS BOMBASTES PARACELSUS AND RAYMOND LULLI WERE THE SAME MAN.

UM. *HELLO?*

IS THERE, UM, ANYONE HERE? HE SAYS-- RIC, UH, SAYS YOU'RE FREE TO GO. *HELLO?*

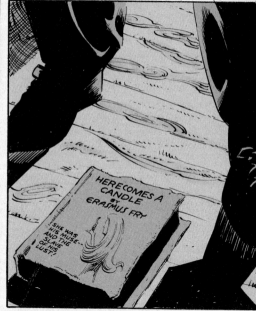

HERE COMES A CANDLE
BY ERASMUS FRY

SHE WAS HIS MUSE-- AND THE SLAVE OF HIS LUST.

22

SO. IT'S OVER. THANK YOU.

WHAT WILL YOU DO NOW, CALLIOPE?

I DON'T KNOW. RETURN TO THE MINDS OF HUMANITY, I SUSPECT. MY TIME IS OVER, AND THIS AGE OF THE WORLD IS NOT MY AGE.

YOU HAVE *CHANGED*, ONEIROS. IN THE OLD DAYS, YOU WOULD HAVE LEFT ME TO ROT FOREVER, WITHOUT TURNING A HAIR...

DO YOU STILL *HATE* ME? FOR WHAT I DID?

No. I no longer hate you, Calliope. I have learned much in recent times, and...

No matter. I do not hate you, child.

I THINK YOU SHOULD RELEASE THE MORTAL NOW. HE *HAS* SET ME FREE...

If that is what you wish, it is done.

MAYBE...

MAYBE I COULD *VISIT* YOU, IN THE DREAM REALM? IT WOULD BE NICE TO SEE YOU AGAIN. PROPERLY. WHAT DO YOU THINK?

I do not think that would be a good idea, Calliope.

NO. *NO*, PERHAPS IT WOULDN'T.

THANK YOU ANYWAY, ONEIROS. I WILL NOT FORGET THIS.

FARE YOU WELL, ONEIROS. *FORTUNE* GO WITH YOU.

Goodbye, Calliope.

(23)

I'VE DONE IT, RIC. UM, HOW ARE YOU FEELING NOW?

I...I DON'T KNOW ANY MORE. I KEEP TRYING TO THINK...ABOUT WHAT SHE SAID...

"THE SHAPER OF FORMS"...IT SEEMS LIKE IT SHOULD *MEAN* SOMETHING...

THERE WAS NO ONE THERE. IN THE ROOM. THERE WAS JUST A BOOK.

I DON'T KNOW...IT DOESN'T CONNECT WITH ANYTHING...IT'S A NAME...

I WISH I COULD REMEMBER.

IT'S SO HARD TO THINK...

...MORPHEUS? ...ORPHEUS?...ONE OF THOSE...

YOU CAN TAKE IT WITH YOU TO THE *HOSPITAL*, RICHARD.

SHE'S GONE, YOU SEE. AND IT'S ALL GONE WITH HER. EVERYTHING. ALL OF THEM, ALL THE DREAMS...

NO...I CAN'T REMEMBER. I'VE LOST IT...

IT'S GONE. I'VE GOT NO IDEA ANY MORE.

NO IDEA AT ALL.

NEXT...   A DREAM OF A THOUSAND CATS

COME ON, DARLING. COME TO BED.

AND LEAVE THE DOOR TO THE KITCHEN OPEN SO THE KITTY CAN GET TO THE LITTER TRAY.

YES, HON.

AW, COME *ON*, DON. IF YOU DON'T GET UP HERE SOON, I WON'T BE IN THE MOOD ANYMORE.

YES, HON.

G'NIGHT, KITTY.

SSS! IT'S TONIGHT!

WHAT?

SHE'S *HERE*. ARE YOU COMING? IT SHOULD BE AMUSING.

I DON'T KNOW HOW I CAN GET OUT. I CAN'T GET THROUGH ANY OF THE WALL OPENINGS.

UP THERE, A CLEAR-HOLE IS PARTLY OPENED. YOU CAN GET OUT THROUGH THERE.

SHAKE YOUR TAIL, LITTLE ONE. WE MUSTN'T MISS THIS.

OHH. CAN YOU NOT *SCENT* IT, CHILD? THE CALL OF THE NIGHT?

HURRY. *HURRY.*

WAIT FOR ME. OH *WAIT* FOR ME, *PLEASE.*

SISTERS. BROTHERS. GOOD HUNTING.

THANK YOU FOR COMING TO LISTEN TO ME; FOR YOUR WILLINGNESS TO HEAR MY MESSAGE.

AND I HOPE THAT WHEN I HAVE FINISHE SOME OF YOU MAY SHARE MY DREAM.

HE WAS STRONG, AND FAST, AND HIS CLAWS AND TEETH WERE SHARP AS WINTER.

OUR PLEASURE IN EACH OTHER, AND THE CONSUMMATION OF OUR MUTUAL HUNGER, WAS SCREECHED TO THE HEAVENS, AND SCREAMED TO THE ARCHES OF THE SKY.

I NEVER SAW HIM AGAIN. BUT I HAVE NOT FORGOTTEN HIM.

IN THE FULLNESS OF TIME, OUR PLEASURE BROUGHT FORTH OFFSPRING, A WONDERFUL UNITY OF BOTH OUR MARKINGS.

I ANTICIPATED THE ZEST WITH WHICH I WOULD TEACH THEM OF LIFE...

...OF THE JOYS OF WASHING, OF HUNTING, OF SURVIVAL.

THEY WHISPERED TO ME THEIR DELIGHT: IN HAVING TAKEN FLESH IN MY BLOODLINE; OF TASTING AIR, AND MILK; WHISPERED THEIR BELIEF IN THE FUTURE.

MY HUMANS DID NOT SHARE OUR JOY.

YOU *KNEW* SHE WAS IN HEAT! WHY THE *HELL* DIDN'T YOU LOCK HER IN?

STOP *COMPLAINING*, PAUL. I THINK THEY'RE KIND OF *CUTE*.

CUTE? SHE'S A PURE-BRED BLUE POINT *SIAMESE!*

THESE LITTLE BUNDLES OF FLUFF AREN'T WORTH *DIDDLY-SQUAT.*

meep.

⑧

I FELT THEM FROM AFAR, IN THE DARK, AS THE COLD WATER TOOK THEM.

FELT THEM THRESH AND CLAW SIGHTLESSLY; FELT THEM CALL ME, IN THEIR PANIC AND THEIR FEAR.

AND THEN THEY WERE GONE.

I KNEW THEN THAT I HAD BEEN FOOLING MYSELF. THAT WE WERE SUBORDINATE. THAT WHILE WE LIVED WITH HUMANITY WE COULD NOT CALL OURSELVES FREE.

AND I PRAYED.

FOR GOD'S SAKE, MARION! IT'S NOT EVEN AS IF SHE UNDERSTANDS. I MEAN, LOOK AT HER. SHE'S PROBABLY RELIEVED.

SHE'S PRACTICALLY A KITTEN HERSELF. SHE WOULD HAVE EXHAUSTED HERSELF...

I'M SURE YOU'RE RIGHT, PAUL. BUT I CAN'T HELP FEELING A LITTLE GUILTY.

9

I PRAYED TO THE DARKNESS, TO THE NIGHT, TO THE *CARRION KIND*.

I PRAYED TO THE KING OF THE CATS, THE KIND'S EMISSARY ON EARTH, HE WHO WALKS AMONGST US AND WE DO NOT KNOW HIM.

I PRAYED...

...AND I *DREAMED*.

WHY HAVE YOU VENTURED TO THE HEART OF THE DREAMING, LITTLE CAT?

THERE IS *NOTHING* HERE FOR YOU.

I HAVE COME HERE FOR *JUSTICE*; I HAVE COME FOR *REVELATION*; I HAVE COME FOR *WISDOM*.

⑩

THE BIRD FLEW LOWER, BUT IT DID NOT COME WITHIN MY REACH.

"JUSTICE?" IT REPEATED. "JUSTICE IS A *DELUSION* YOU WILL NOT FIND ON *THIS* OR ANY OTHER SPHERE."

"AND *WISDOM?* WISDOM IS NO *PART* OF *DREAMS,* LITHE WALKER, THOUGH DREAMS ARE A PART OF THE SUM OF EACH LIFE'S EXPERIENCES, WHICH IS THE *ONLY* WISDOM THAT MATTERS."

BUT *REVELATION?*

THAT IS THE PROVINCE OF DREAM.

IT *CAN* BE YOURS, BUT ONLY IF YOUR HEART IS STRONG.

DO YOU SEE THAT *MOUNTAIN?* IN THAT MOUNTAIN IS A CAVE, AND IN THAT CAVE LIVES THE *CAT OF DREAMS,* THE RULER OF THIS SLEEPING WORLD.

SEEK HIM OUT. BUT *BEWARE.* THE WAY TO HIS CAVE IS HARD, AND A LITTLE CAT COULD COME TO MUCH HARM.

ALL PLACES ARE THE SAME TO ME. I WILL FIND THE CAVE, THEN, AND FIND MY ANSWERS.

I AM NOT AFRAID.

THEN FARE YOU WELL, DAUGHTER.

AND I LEFT THE DESERT OF BONES, AND I BEGAN THE LONG JOURNEY TO THE HOME OF THE CAT OF DREAMS.

11

I WALKED THROUGH THE WOOD OF GHOSTS, WHERE THE DEAD AND THE LOST WHISPERED CONTINUALLY, PROMISED ME WORLDS IF I WOULD ONLY STOP AND PLAY WITH THEM.

I CLOSED MY EARS TO THEIR ENTREATIES.

AT ONE POINT I THOUGHT I HEARD MY CHILDREN CALLING ME. BUT I STRAIGHTENED MY TAIL, AND I WALKED FORWARD.

I WALKED THROUGH THE COLD PLACES, HARD AND FROZEN, WHERE EVERY STEP WAS PAIN, EVERY MOVEMENT WAS TORMENT.

I WALKED ON.

I WALKED THROUGH THE WETNESS THAT NUMBED MY PAWS, DRENCHED MY FUR, TRIED TO WASH AWAY MY MEMORIES.

I WALKED THROUGH THE DARKNESS, THROUGH THE VOID, WHERE EVERYTHING WAS SUCKED FROM ME--EVERYTHING THAT MAKES ME WHAT I AM.

BUT EVEN IN THE EMPTINESS OF PURE NOTHING, NO LONGER KNOWING WHY I WAS WALKING OR WHAT I WAS SEEKING, I WALKED ONWARD.

AND, AFTER A TIME, MY SELF RETURNED TO ME, AND I LEFT THAT PLACE, AND I FOUND MYSELF AT THE MOUNTAIN OF THE CAT OF DREAMS.

12

THE SCENT ON THE AIR WAS STRANGE, BUT STILL IT WAS CAT.

I WALKED FORWARD SLOWLY, EVERY SENSE SCREAMING AT ME TO FLEE THIS PLACE. MY FUR PRICKLED, MY CLAWS EXTENDED.

AND THEN I STOOD BEFORE HIM.

Walk with me, then, little sister, and tell me why you have sought me out.

I AM HERE.

And who might you be?

A *CAT*. A WALKER IN NIGHT PLACES. A DEAD CROW SENT ME HERE, FOR REVELATION.

I HOPED I SOUNDED CONFIDENT, BUT TRULY I WAS SCARED.

I... I WANT TO *UNDERSTAND*.

WHY COULD THEY TAKE MY CHILDREN FROM ME? *WHY* DO WE LIVE AS WE DO? I DON'T *UNDERSTAND*.

A cat may look at a king, or so they say.

Look into my eyes then, little sister.

Look into my eyes.

14

AND IT SHOWED ME. IT TOLD ME THE TRUTH, EVEN AS I AM TELLING IT TO YOU NOW.

FOR IN ITS EYES I SAW PICTURES. AND IN THE PICTURES I SAW THE *TRUTH.*

ALL CATS CAN SEE FUTURES, AND SEE ECHOES OF THE PAST. WE CAN WATCH THE PASSAGE OF CREATURES FROM THE INFINITY OF NOW, FROM ALL THE WORLDS LIKE OURS, ONLY FRACTIONALLY DIFFERENT.

AND WE FOLLOW THEM WITH OUR EYES, GHOST THINGS, AND THE HUMANS SEE NOTHING.

BUT THE REALITY THE CAT OF DREAMS SHOWED ME TRANSCENDED ANYTHING I HAD IMAGINED.

MANY, MANY SEASONS AGO, CATS TRULY RULED THIS WORLD.

WE WERE LARGER THEN, AND THIS WHOLE WORLD WAS CREATED FOR OUR PLEASURE. WE ROAMED IT AS WE WOULD, TAKING WHAT WE WANTED.

15

IN THOSE TIMES HUMANS WERE TINY CREATURES, NO LARGER THAN WE ARE NOW.

AND THE HUMANS WOULD GROOM US, AND FEED US, AND PET US.

AND WHEN THE MOON SHONE FULL, WE WOULD *HUNT* THEM, AND WE WOULD EAT *PART* OF THEM, BUT CHIEFLY WE WOULD HUNT THEM...

...FOR THEY WERE MORE DELIGHTFUL TO HUNT EVEN THAN BIRDS, AND BACK THEN, MICE WERE TOO SMALL AND INSIGNIFICANT FOR US TO DEIGN TO TOUCH.

OH, THE *JOY* OF THOSE HUNTING DAYS, BENEATH THE CAT'S MOON. THE *GAME* OF *CAT* AND *MAN*...

PRRRRRR.

16

THEN A HUMAN AROSE AMONGST THEM. A GOLDEN-FURRED MALE, BRED AND RAISED IN THE PLEASURE GARDENS OF ONE OF THE SYBARITIC FELINE LADIES.

AND THE HUMAN HAD A DREAM, AND AN INSPIRATION. AND IT WALKED AMONGST ITS FELLOWS, AND IT TOLD THEM...

DREAM!

DREAMS SHAPE THE WORLD.

DREAMS CREATE THE WORLD ANEW, *EVERY* NIGHT.

DO *NOT* DREAM THE WORLD THE WAY IT IS *NOW*, IN THRALL TO OUR FELINE MASTERS AND MISTRESSES.

DREAM A *NEW* WORLD. DREAM A WORLD OF *HUMAN BEINGS.* DREAM A WORLD IN WHICH *WE* ARE THE DOMINANT SPECIES, IN WHICH *WE* ARE THE *KINGS* AND THE *QUEENS,* AND THE *GODS.*

DREAM A WORLD IN WHICH WE WILL *NO LONGER* BE *HUNTED* AND *KILLED* BY *CATS.*

I DO NOT KNOW *HOW* MANY OF US IT WILL TAKE. BUT WE *MUST* DREAM IT, AND IF *ENOUGH* OF US DREAM IT, THEN IT *WILL HAPPEN.*

DREAMS *SHAPE* THE *WORLD.*

17

AND THE WORD SPREAD AMONGST THE HUMANS.

AND SOME OF THEM BELIEVED. AND THEY DREAMED.

AND, FOR A WHILE, NOTHING HAPPENED.

ONE NIGHT, ENOUGH OF THEM DREAMED. IT DID NOT TAKE MANY OF THEM. A *THOUSAND*, PERHAPS. NO MORE.

THEY DREAMED...

AND THE NEXT DAY, THINGS CHANGED.

HUMANS WERE HUGE, AND CATS WERE TINY. HUMANS WERE THE DOMINANT SPECIES, AND WE WERE PREY TO THEM, TO DOGS, TO THEIR METAL MACHINES.

PREY TO THE WORLD THE HUMANS HAD BROUGHT WITH THEM.

18

ALL THIS I SAW, WHEN I LOOKED INTO THE DREAM CAT'S EYES.

SO THEY DREAMED THE WORLD INTO THE FORM IT IS NOW?

Not exactly.

They dreamed the world so it ALWAYS WAS the way it is now, little one. There never WAS a world of high cat-ladies and cat-lords.

They changed the universe from the beginning of all things, until the end of time.

Do you understand now?

YES.

YES, I DO.

Then you know what your task must be. You know the burden you must bear.

Are you strong enough?

YES. I HOPE SO.

"Then wake, child. With my blessing."

19

YOU SEE, I HAD SEEN THE UNDER-SIDE OF WHAT HE HAD GIVEN TO ME.

IF *THEY* COULD DREAM IT...

WE COULD CHANGE THINGS *BACK.* IF WE *BELIEVED.* IF WE *DREAMED.*

WE ARE THE *DREAMS* OF THE *CARRION KIND,* THEY SAY, AND PERHAPS IT IS SO.

BUT IF *ENOUGH* OF *US* DREAM...

IF A BARE *THOUSAND* OF US DREAM...

...WE CAN *CHANGE* THE *WORLD.*

WE CAN DREAM IT *ANEW!* A WORLD IN WHICH *NO* CAT *SUFFERS* FROM THE MALICE OF HUMANS. IN WHICH *NO* CATS ARE *KILLED* BY HUMAN CAPRICE.

A *WORLD* THAT *WE* RULE.

20

SHE WAS *AMUSING*. I'LL SAY *THAT* FOR HER.

NO, IT FELT *RIGHT*. IT *FELT* LIKE THE *TRUTH*. OR A TRUTH, ANYWAY.

DO YOU THINK IT WILL *HAPPEN?*

MMM. NICE PLUMP RAT.

LITTLE ONE, I WOULD LIKE TO SEE *ANYONE*-- PROPHET, KING OR *GOD*--PERSUADE A THOUSAND CATS TO DO *ANYTHING* AT THE SAME TIME.

NO, IT WILL *NEVER* HAPPEN.

"COME ON, SMALL FRY. THE SUN WILL RISE SOON. WE HAD BETTER GET YOU HOME."

23

NEXT: A MIDSUMMER NIGHT'S DREAM...

A Midsummer Nights Dream.

HOLD FAST! WE STOP HERE, MY FRIENDS.

HAMNET, GO AND WAIT WITH CONDELL AND THE OTHER BOYS.

BUT FATHER...

You have come, then, Will Shekespear.

It is all ready?

I WROTE IT AS YOU TOLD ME, LORD. IT IS THE BEST THAT I HAVE WRITTEN, TO THIS DATE.

I am sure it is.

SO... WE ARE HERE ON YOUR COMMAND, MY LORD, ON MIDSUMMER'S EVE, BY THE LONG MAN OF WILMINGTON. AN ODD CHOICE OF A PLACE FOR US TO PERFORM...

Odd? Wendel's Mound was a theatre before your race came to this island.

BEFORE THE NORMANS?

Before the humans.

2

WILL! WHAT IS HAPPENING? WHO IS THIS MAN?

THIS IS THE *GENTLEMAN* I TOLD YOU OF, RICHARD. IT WAS *HE* WHO COMMISSIONED THE NEW PLAY.

AH. I AM RICHARD BURBAGE, THE LEADING MAN OF LORD STRANGE'S MEN, AND *HEAD* OF OUR COMPANY. AND *YOU* ARE...?

I am your patron, for this play. You must Act well tonight, Richard Burbage.

SIRRAH--I *NEVER* GIVE OF A PERFORMANCE THAT IS LESS THAN MY *BEST.* ALTHOUGH THIS BARBAROUS FARRAGO OF FAIRY-TALE HODGEPOTCH IS A MERE *CROWD-PLEASER* AT BEST.

TRAGEDY IS MY FORTE. I HAVE TOLD WILL TO MAKE ME A LOVER MOST TRAGICAL, AND WHEN WE RETURN TO *LONDON,* I WILL MAKE THEM WEEP TRUE TEARS.

I have no doubts of your ability, Master Burbage.

I SEE YOU UNDERSTAND THE THEATRE, MESSIRE. *LEAD* US TO YOUR *HALL,* THEN, AND WE SHALL PERFORM OUR COMEDY FOR YOUR ENJOYMENT.

I have no hall, not that I will take you to.

Here, Richard Burbage, on the downs of Sussex, this will be your stage.

BUT--

WE WILL *PLAY* IT ON THE GREEN SWARD, RICHARD, JUST AS WE HAVE *REHEARSED* IT IN FIELDS AND GLADES. THIS IS A *NATURAL* STAGE. AND THE EVENING IS WARM, AND THE LIGHT WILL LAST US.

WE OWE-- I OWE *MUCH* TO THIS MAN.

BESTIR YOURSELVES THERE, *LUMPKINS!* AND INTO YOUR *COSTUMES!* WE PERFORM THE PLAY HERE, ON THIS GREEN, WITHIN THE *HOUR.*

HMMPH.

3

I CAN'T *WAIT* UNTIL WE'RE BACK IN THE SMOKE. I *LOATHE* THESE PROVINCIAL TOURS.

AS SOON AS THE PLAGUE SEASON IS OVER, WE'LL BE BACK AT THE *CURTAIN,* AND THE *CROSS KEYS,* AND YOU CAN MAKE UP TO *ALL* YOUR ADMIRERS AGAIN...

COW. AT LEAST I *HAVE* ADMIRERS.

MY FATHER SAYS IT'S NOT THE PLAGUE THAT'S THE PROBLEM, IT'S THE CITY ALDERMEN.

YES, DO ME UP IN THE BACK, THERE'S A LOVE.

DID YOUR FATHER SAY WHO THAT STRANGER IS? OR WHO WE'LL BE PERFORMING FOR?

NO.

HOW DO I LOOK?

YOU LOOK *VERY* PRETTY.

THANK YOU, HAMNET. FOR THAT, YOU SHALL HAVE A STRAWBERRY.

WHO HAS MOVED THE ASS'S HEAD?

WHERE'S THE LANTHORN? AND THE STICKS?

MY BEARD! BY TH' LORD JESU! Y'ART WEARING MY BEARD!

THE KING DOTH KEEP HIS REVELS HERE TONIGHT MARK NOT-- I'FAITH -- *TAKE HEED* THE QUEEN COME NOT WITHIN HIS SIGHT...

SIRE, ALL IS PREPARED, AND WE POOR PLAYERS BUT AWAIT OUR CUES.

ARE OUR AUDIENCE ON THEIR WAY?

They wait on the other side of the hill, needing only the unclosing of a portal to make their way to us.

I will call them. Go tell your fellow players to make ready to begin.

Wendel! Open your door.

4

A MIDSUMMER NIGHT'S DREAM

Written by **NEIL GAIMAN**, with additional material taken from the play by **WILLIAM SHAKESPEARE**. Art by **CHARLES VESS**.
Colored by **STEVE OLIFF** Lettered by **TODD KLEIN**. Assistant Editor **TOM PEYER**. Editor **KAREN BERGER**.
featuring characters created by **GAIMAN, KIETH & DRINGENBERG**.

5

HO HO *HO!* THEY SAY THE SEVEN ENDLESS ARE FOREVER, MIGHTY DREAM. YOU AND THE OTHER SIX, UNTIL THE DEATH OF TIME ITSELF.

WHAT SAY YOU TO THAT, KING OF THE RIDDLE-REALMS?

ROBIN GOODFELLOW, MIND YOUR MANNERS. WE ARE MY LORD SHAPER'S GUESTS, AND I WILL *NOT* HAVE HIM INSULTED BY A HOBGOBLIN.

Welcome to you, Auberon of Dom-Daniel, and to you also, Lady Titania.

Nay, good Auberon. It is a fool's prerogative to utter truths that no one else will speak.

Please, take your seats. The diversion I have arranged begins forthwith.

GREETINGS, SHAPER. YOUR INVITATION HAS PROVOK'D MUCH SPECULATION AMONGST OUR PEOPLE. I MUST CONFESS WE THOUGHT WE WERE *QUIT* OF THIS PLANE FOR *EVER.*

Is anything forever?

FATHER-- THEY ARE ALL ASSEMBLED.

VERY WELL.

LET *THIS* OUR FIRST PERFORMANCE BE OUR *BEST,* MY FRIENDS. *WILL KEMP--NO* BUSINESS WE HAVE NOT REHEARSED. *HENRY CONDELL,* REMEMBER THAT YOU PLAY A *QUEEN,* NOT A *STRUMPET.*

HIPPOLYTA-- PHILOSTRATE-- PLACES.

AND...BREAK A LEG.

6

...

"NOW, FAIR HIPPOLYTA..."

NOW, FAIR HIPPOLYTA, OUR NUPTIAL HOUR DRAWS ON APACE; *FOUR* HAPPY DAYS BRING IN ANOTHER MOON: BUT *OHH*, METHINKS HOW *SLOW* THE OLD MOON WANES!

...AWAKE THE PERT AND NIMBLE SPIRIT OF MIRTH; TURN MELANCHOLY FORTH TO FUNERALS -- THE *PALE COMPANION* IS *NOT* FOR OUR POMP.

7

EITHER *I* MISTAKE YOUR SHAPE AND MAKING *QUITE*, OR ELSE *YOU* ARE THAT *SHREWD* AND *KNAVISH* SPRITE CALLED *ROBIN GOODFELLOW*:

ARE YOU NOT *HE* THAT FRIGHTS THE MAIDENS OF THE VILLAGERY...?

IT'S *YOU!* HOBGOBLIN, THAT ACTOR PERSONATES *YOU!*

THOU SPEAK'ST ARIGHT: *I AM* THAT MERRY WANDERER OF THE NIGHT.

"*I AM THAT MERRY WANDERER OF THE NIGHT*"? I AM THAT GIGGLING-DANGEROUS-TOTALLY-BLOODY-PSYCHOTIC-MENACE-TO-LIFE-AND-LIMB, MORE LIKE IT.

SHUSH, PEASEBLOSSOM. THE PUCK MIGHT *HEAR* YOU!

IT SEEMS TO ME THAT I HEARD THIS TALE SUNG ONCE, IN OLD GREECE, BY A BOY WITH A LYRE.

Indeed, my lady?

YOU ARE A DEEP ONE. I WOULD I COULD FATHOM YOUR MOTIVES...?

Later, lady. Watch the play.

ILL-MET BY *MOONLIGHT*, PROUD TITANIA.

WHAT, JEALOUS OBERON? FAIRY, SKIP HENCE. I HAVE FORSWORN HIS *BED* AND *COMPANY*.

TARRY, RASH WANTON! AM I NOT THY LORD?

10

...BUT SHE, BEING MORTAL OF THAT BOY DID *DIE*, AND FOR HER SAKE I DO *REAR UP* HER *BOY*; AND FOR HER SAKE I WILL *NOT* PART WITH HIM.

THAT CHILD-- THE ONE PLAYING THE INDIAN BOY. WHO *IS* HE?

He is the son of Will Shekespear, the author of this play.

...THE NEXT THING THEN SHE, WAKING, LOOKS UPON--BE IT ON LION, BEAR, OR WOLF, OR BULL, ON MEDDLING MONKEY, OR ON BUSY APE--

SHE SHALL PURSUE IT WITH THE SOUL OF *LOVE*.

A *BEAUTIFUL* CHILD. MOST PLEASANT. WILL I MEET HIM?

I have told Shekespear to call an interval, half-way through the play; and you will meet him then.

AHH. 'TIS UNCOMMON FOR YOU TO HAVE SUCH WAKING COMMERCE WITH MORTAL KIND...?

We came to an...arrangement, four years back. I'd give him what he thinks he most desires-- and in return he'd write two plays for me.

This is the first of them.

I UNDERSTAND.

SO.

WE HAVE FOUR LOVERS HEADING FOR THE WOOD. WE HAVE CLOWNS, WHO WOULD BE ACTORS; AND ACTORS PORTRAYING ME AND MY ROYAL CONSORT.

IN THE OLD TALE THERE WAS A LOVE POTION, THAT LEFT THE GODDESS RUTTING WITH AN ASS...

AH YES. THE LOVE POTION.

⑪

STAY-- THOUGH THOU KILL ME, SWEET DEMETRIUS.

I CHARGE THEE HENCE-- AND DO NOT *HAUNT* ME THUS!

O, WILT THOU DARKLING LEAVE ME? DO *NOT* GO!

STAY, ON THY PERIL. I ALONE WILL GO.

HANG ON. SO THERE'S THIS LOVE POTION, AND HE'S GOIN' TO MAKE HER MAJESTY LOVE SOMETHING NASTY... BUT WHERE DO THE YOUNG MORTALS COME INTO IT?

DON'T YOU *EVER* LISSEN? *HE'S* PUT THE POTION ON WOSSNAME, *LYSANDER*, RIGHT? *NOW* HE'S GOING TO FALL IN LOVE WITH *HER*, THE SKINNY ONE.

HUH?

YOU SEE, THE PUCK THOUGHT *HE* WAS THE OTHER ONE, SO WHEN--

CAN'T YOU BE QUIET? *SOME* OF US ARE TRYING TO LISTEN.

NOT HERMIA BUT HELENA I LOVE-- WHO WOULD NOT CHANGE A RAVEN FOR A DOVE?

THE PLAY GOES *WELL*, WILL. *HOWEVER*, IT SEEMS TO ME THAT WE ARE PERFORMING FOR SIMPLE APPLAUSE. AND EVEN WE GLORIOUS VAGABONDS MUST *EAT*.

WE SHALL HAVE AN INTERVAL, AT THE END OF KEMP AND CONDELL'S FIRST SCENE. WE CAN TALK OF SILVER THEN.

AY ME! FOR PITY! WHAT A *DREAM* WAS *HERE!* LYSANDER, LOOK HOW I DO QUAKE WITH FEAR!

METHOUGHT A SERPENT ATE MY *HEART* AWAY, AND YOU STOOD *SMILING* AT HIS CRUEL PREY.

LYSANDER...?

12

YOU MUST BE VERY PROUD OF YOUR FATHER, HAMNET.

PROUD? I SUPPOSE...

HE'S VERY DISTANT, TOMMY. HE DOESN'T SEEM LIKE HE'S REALLY *THERE* ANY MORE. NOT REALLY. IT'S LIKE HE'S SOMEWHERE ELSE. ANYTHING THAT HAPPENS HE JUST MAKES *STORIES* OUT OF IT.

I'M LESS REAL TO HIM THAN ANY OF THE CHARACTERS IN HIS PLAYS.

MOTHER SAYS HE'S *CHANGED* IN THE LAST FIVE YEARS, BUT I DON'T REMEMBER HIM ANY OTHER WAY. *JUDITH*-- SHE'S MY TWIN SISTER-- SHE ONCE JOKED THAT IF I *DIED,* HE'D JUST WRITE A *PLAY* ABOUT IT.

"HAMNET."

COME ON, LADDIE. I AM BACK *ON* IN A MINUTE!

MOTHER *ORDERED* HIM TO HAVE ME FOR THIS SUMMER. IT'S THE *FIRST* TIME I'VE SEEN HIM FOR *MORE* THAN A *WEEK* AT A TIME, THAT I REMEMBER.

BUT WE LIVE FIVE DAYS' RIDE FROM LONDON, UP IN WARWICKSHIRE, AND SEE HIM SELDOM.

ALL THAT MATTERS TO HIM...

I WOULD BE *PROUD* OF HIM, IF HE WERE *MY* FATHER.

...ALL THAT MATTERS IS THE STORIES.

I'LL FOLLOW YOU, I'LL LEAD YOU ABOUT, AROUND, THROUGH BUSH, THROUGH BRAKE, THROUGH BRIAR.

SOMETIME A *HORSE* I'LL BE, SOMETIME A *HOUND*--

--A *HOG,* A HEADLESS *BEAR,* SOMETIME A *FIRE*...

WHY DO THEY RUN AWAY?

THIS IS A KNAVERY OF THEM TO MAKE *ME* A-FEARED!

THIS IS *MAGNIFICENT*-- AND IT IS *TRUE!*

IT NEVER *HAPPENED;* YET IT IS *STILL* TRUE. WHAT MAGIC ART IS THIS?

13

WHAT *ANGEL* WAKES ME FROM MY FLOWERY BED?

ALL RIGHT. WHAT'S SO FUNNY ABOUT HAVING A DONKEY'S HEAD? EH? *EH?*

GO ON, *TELL* ME WHAT'S SO *FUNNY?*

...I LOVE THEE.

METHINKS, MISTRESS, YOU SHOULD HAVE *LITTLE* REASON FOR *THAT.*

AND YET, TO SAY THE TRUTH, *REASON* AND *LOVE* KEEP LITTLE COMPANY TOGETHER NOWADAYS.

BESIDES--IF YOU ASK *ME, NONE* OF THOSE *WOMEN* ARE WOMEN AT ALL. THEY'RE MALES. *I* CAN TELL.

HUMAN MALES TASTE MORE LIKE *RABBIT* THAN THE FEMALES --AND THEY *STICK* IN YOUR *TEETH.* OH YES.

DID HE SAY "PEASEBLOSSOM"? THAT'S *MY* NAME! WHAT DID HE *SAY?*

ALSO, THE MALES ARE *HAIRIER,* AND THEY LACK THE FLESH ON THEIR *CHESTS.*

WILL YOU *SHUT UP?* I CAN'T HEAR A *THING* WITH YOU RABBITIN' ON LIKE THAT ALL THE TIME!

GENTLES, THERE WILL NOW BE INTERVAL, FOR YOU TO FRESHEN, OR TO STRETCH YOUR LEGS.

OUR TALE BEGINS AGAIN TEN MINUTES HENCE.

14

YOU ARE THE AUTHOR OF THIS AMUSEMENT? IT STRIKES STRANGE MUSIC, SIR. METHINKS I SHOULD BE DISPLEASED, YET I AM NOT.

IT IS FINE WORK. IT IS MOST WORTHY WORK.

AND, UM, THESE -- NO -- THOSE THINGS DO BEST PLEASE ME THAT BEFALL PREPOSTEROUSLY.

AND PUCK MEETS PUCK -- IS THAT NOT PREPOSTEROUS? AND WHAT'S THIS I SPY? YOUR LINES?

OHO-HO-HO, I DO SEE SPORT HERE..

MY LORD. I AM THE, UH, LEADER OF THESE, LORD STRANGE'S MEN. AND THOUGH IT IS A JOY FOR US TO PERFORM, WE ALSO NEED TO PAY OUR WAY THROUGH THE COUNTRYSIDE.

YOU TALK OF GOLD?

WELL, YES...

GOLD. YOU ASK AUBERON OF THE FAY FOR GOLD...?

THEN YOU MUST HAVE YOUR GOLD, ACTOR.

WHY, THANK YOU, LORD! THIS WILL BE MORE THAN SUFFICIENT!

YOU PLAYED ME WELL, MORTAL. BUT I HAVE PLAYED ME FOR TIME OUT OF MIND.

AND I DO ROBIN GOODFELLOW BETTER THAN ANYONE.

15

They are well pleased, as am I, good Will. It is finely crafted, and it will last.

ARE YOU SATISFIED?

I am.

IF YOU ARE SATISFIED, THEN OUR BARGAIN IS HALF-CONCLUDED.

ONE OTHER PLAY THEN, CELEBRATING DREAMS, AT THE END OF MY CAREER...

YES, "THE DREAM" IS THE BEST THING I HAVE WRITTEN; AND IT PLAYS WELL. NOT EVEN KIT MARLOWE WILL BE ABLE TO GAINSAY THAT.

You have not heard? Marlowe is dead, Will. He died in Deptford, three weeks back, of a knife wound to the head.

WHO KILLED HIM? INGRAM FRASER, I'LL BE BOUND. CECIL'S MAN.

Yes.

OH, KIT. I TOLD YOU NOT TO PLAY WITH POLITICS.

WHY DID YOU TELL THIS TO ME NOW? THIS NEWS COULD HAVE WAITED.

MARLOWE WAS MY FRIEND.

I did not realize it would hurt you so.

YOU DID NOT REALIZE? NO, YOUR KIND CARE NOT FOR HUMAN LIVES.

DARK STRANGER, ALREADY I HALF-REGRET OUR BARGAIN. BUT COME, OUR NIGHT'S COMEDY BEGINS ONCE MORE.

...AND BONNY DRAGONS THAT WILL COME WHEN YOU DO CALL THEM AND FLY YOU THROUGH THE HONEYED AMBER SKIES.

THERE IS NO NIGHT IN MY LAND, PRETTY BOY, AND IT IS FOREVER SUMMER'S TWILIGHT.

My lady? The play will start anon.

THANK YOU, DREAM LORD.

16

HOW NOW, MAD SPIRIT? WHAT *NIGHT-RULE* NOW ABOUT THIS HAUNTED GROVE?

MY *MISTRESS* WITH A *MONSTER* IS IN LOVE!

THIS MUST BE OUR *LAST* VISIT TO THIS EARTH, SHAPER.

THINGS HAVE CHANGED, AND WILL CHANGE *MORE*; AND GAIA NO LONGER WELCOMES US AS ONCE SHE DID.

I know. And I regret it much.

BUT *YOU* WILL *ALWAYS* BE WELCOME IN *OUR* LAND, DREAM LORD. THE GATES TO FAERIE ARE NEVER *FULLY* CLOSED. COME WHEN YOU WISH.

Perhaps one day I will.

DICK COWLEY ACTS WELL TONIGHT. I HAVE NEVER SEEN HIM FEIGN A FINER PUCK.

HE SEEMS ALMOST TWO-THIRDS HOBGOBLIN.

father?

NOT NOW, CHILD. I MUST SEE THIS.

SHE WAS SUCH A *PRETTY* LADY, FATHER, AND SHE SAID SUCH THINGS TO ME.

LORD, WHAT *FOOLS* THESE *MORTALS* BE!

17

COME, SIT THEE DOWN UPON THIS FLOWERY BED, WHILE I THY AMIABLE CHEEKS DO COY, AND STICK MUSKROSES IN THY SLEEK, SMOOTH HEAD, --

--AND *KISS* THY FAIR LARGE EARS, MY GENTLE JOY.

WHERE'S *PEASEBLOSSOM?*

READY!

SCRATCH MY HEAD, PEASEBLOSSOM.

DID YOU *HEAR* THAT? *PEASEBLOSSOM!* THAT'S MEANT TO BE *ME*, THAT IS! ISS NUFFINK *LIKE* ME! *NUFFINK!*

IT *ISN'T* YOU, PEASE BLOSSOM. NOW BE QUIET.

YER. YOU SHUT YOUR FACE, PEASE.

ISSA *WOSSNAME*. TRAVELOGUE? NAH. *TRAVESTY.* THAT'S IT.

I'M THE ONLY PEASEBLOSSOM AMONG THE FAY. "SCRATCH *HIS* HEAD". I'LL GIVE HIM SCRATCH HIS BLEEDIN' HEAD!

PEASEBLOSSOM...

...AND *NOW* I HAVE THE BOY I WILL *UNDO* THIS HATEFUL IMPERFECTION OF HER EYES.

AND, GENTLE PUCK, TAKE THIS TRANSFORMED SCALP FROM OFF THE HEAD OF THIS ATHENIAN SWAIN.

MMMPH! MUMUMPH MM MPPH!

LIKE I SAID. I'M NOT HAVIN' YOU SPOILIN' IT FOR EVERYONE.

⑱

I HAVE HAD...A MOST *RARE* VISION.

I HAVE HAD A *DREAM*...PAST THE WIT OF MAN TO SAY WHAT WIT IT WAS.

MAN IS BUT AN...ASS,,, IF HE GO ABOUT TO EXPOUND THIS DREAM.

METHOUGHT I WAS...THERE IS NO *MAN* CAN TELL WHAT.

I wonder, Titania. I wonder if I have done right.

And I wonder why I wonder. Will is a willing vehicle for the great stories.

Through him they will live for an age of man; and his words will echo down through time. It is what he wanted.

But he did not understand the price. Mortals never do.

They only *see* the prize, their heart's desire, their dream... But the price of getting what you want, is getting what once you wanted.

And had I told him? Had he understood? What then? It would have made no difference.

Have I done right, Titania? Have I done right?

HM? OH, IT IS A *WONDERFUL* PLAY, LORD SHAPER. MOST ENCHANTING AND FINE.

THE *EYE* OF MAN HATH *NOT HEARD*, THE *EAR* OF MAN HATH NOT *SEEN*, MAN'S *HAND* IS NOT ABLE TO *TASTE*, HIS *TONGUE* TO *CONCEIVE*, NOR HIS *HEART* TO *REPORT* WHAT MY DREAM WAS.

'TIS STRANGE, MY THESEUS, THAT THESE LOVERS SPEAK OF.

MORE *STRANGE* THAN *TRUE*.

I NEVER MAY BELIEVE THESE ANTIQUE FABLES, NOR THESE *FAIRY* TOYS. LOVERS AND MADMEN HAVE SUCH *SEETHING* BRAINS...

THE *LUNATIC*, THE *LOVER*, AND THE *POET* ARE OF IMAGINATION ALL COMPACT. *ONE* SEES MORE DEVILS THAN VAST HELL CAN HOLD.

THAT IS THE *MADMAN*.

THE LOVER, ALL AS FRANTIC, SEES HELEN'S BEAUTY IN A BROW OF EGYPT.

THE POET'S EYE, IN A FINE *FRENZY* ROLLING, DOTH GLANCE FROM HEAVEN TO EARTH, FROM EARTH TO HEAVEN.

AND, AS *IMAGINATION* BODIES FORTH THE FORMS OF THINGS UNKNOWN...

...THE POET'S PEN TURNS THEM TO SHAPES, AND GIVES TO AIRY *NOTHING* A LOCAL HABITATION AND A *NAME*.

"THE RIOT OF THE TIPSY BACCHANALS, TEARING THE THRACIAN SINGER IN THEIR RAGE?"

THAT IS AN *OLD* DEVICE, AND IT WAS PLAYED WHEN I FROM THEBES CAME *LAST* A *CONQUEROR*.

20

OH *KISS* ME THROUGH THE HOLE OF THIS VILE WALL!

I *KISS* THE WALL'S *HOLE*, NOT YOUR LIPS AT ALL!

You have asked me why I asked you back to this plane, to see this entertainment.

I... During your stay on this Earth the faerie have afforded me much diversion, and entertainment.

Now you have left, for your own haunts. And I would repay you all for the amusement. And more:

They shall not forget you. That was important to me: that King Auberon and Queen Titania will be remembered by mortals, until this age is gone.

WE THANK YOU, SHAPER. BUT THIS DIVERSION, ALTHOUGH PLEASANT, IS NOT *TRUE*.

THINGS NEVER HAPPENED THUS.

Oh, but it IS true.

Things need not have happened to be true. Tales and dreams are the shadow-truths that will endure when mere facts are dust and ashes, and forgot.

IF YOU SAY SO, DREAM LORD. WE ARE *HONORED*.

THIS IS THE *SILLIEST* STUFF THAT *EVER* I HEARD.

THE *BEST* IN THIS KIND ARE BUT *SHADOWS*; AND THE *WORST* ARE NO *WORSE*, IF *IMAGINATION* AMEND THEM.

(21)

THE IRON TONGUE OF MIDNIGHT HATH TOLLED TWELVE. LOVERS, TO BED; 'TIS ALMOST FAIRY TIME.

I FEAR WE SHALL OUTSLEEP THE COMING MORN...

... WE FAIRIES, THAT DO RUN BY THE TRIPLE HECATE'S TEAM, FOLLOWING DARKNESS LIKE A DREAM, NOW ARE FROLIC.

COME, MY PUCK, AND *LEAVE* THIS FOOLISHNESS, FOR NOW THE TIME FOR OUR *RETURN* DRAWS NEAR.

ALREADY WENDEL OPENS UP HIS GATE.

WHAT, *LEAVE*, MY LORD?

WHEN THERE ARE *MORTALS* TO *CONFUSTICATE* AND *VEX*?

GO YOU ALL. YOUR PUCK WILL STAY--THE LAST HOBGOBLIN IN A DREARY WORLD. HO HO *HO*!

Goodbye, King and Queen. Fare well, fair folk. Go in peace.

THAT IS NOT COWLEY! WHAT'S HAPPENING? WHERE ARE THEY GOING?

WHAT'S *HAPPENING*?

IF WE *SHADOWS* HAVE OFFENDED, THINK BUT *THIS*, AND ALL IS *MENDED*:

THAT YOU HAVE BUT *SLUMBER'D* HERE, WHILE THESE *VISIONS* DID APPEAR.

AND THIS WEAK AND IDLE THEME, NO MORE YIELDING THAN A *DREAM*. GENTLES -- DO NOT REPREHEND. IF *YOU* PARDON-- *WE* WILL MEND.

AND -- AS I AM AN *HONEST* PUCK, IF WE HAVE UNEARNED *LUCK* NOW TO 'SCAPE THE SERPENTS' TONGUE, WE WILL MAKE AMENDS, ERE LONG.

ELSE THE PUCK A LIAR CALL.

SO *GOOD NIGHT* UNTO YOU ALL.

GIVE ME YOUR *HANDS* IF WE BE FRIENDS

AND

ROBIN

SHALL

RESTORE

AMENDS

23

OHH...

WAS IT A DREAM, THEN, RICHARD?

A *DREAM*, WILL? *NO!*

FOR SEE-- A POUCH OF GOLD.

A POUCH OF YELLOW LEAVES.

BUT-- WE WERE *CHEATED!*

NO, FOR WE WERE PAID FULL WELL. *WHICH* OTHER TROUPE HAS PLAYED TO SUCH AN AUDIENCE?

FATHER! I HAD SUCH A STRANGE DREAM. THERE WAS A GREAT LADY, WHO WANTED ME TO GO WITH HER TO A DISTANT LAND...

FOOLISH FANCIES, BOY.

ON THE CART TODAY, YOU MUST PRACTICE YOUR HANDWRITING. PERHAPS YOU COULD WRITE A *LETTER* TO YOUR MOTHER, OR TO JUDITH.

COME ON, YOU *VAGABONDS!* STIR YOURSELVES!

WE CAN BE IN *LEWES* BY LATE AFTERNOON, AND THERE'S AN INN I KNOW WILL BE *GLAD* OF A TROUPE OF ACTORS WITH A NEW COMEDY TO SHOW...

HAMNET SHAKESPEARE DIED IN 1596, AGED ELEVEN.

ROBIN GOODFELLOW'S PRESENT WHEREABOUTS ARE UNKNOWN.

i smoke a cigarette, and i pretend i'm normal. And i wish i were dead.

FAÇADE

THEY SAY THAT CIGARETTES WILL KILL YOU, EVENTUALLY.

FINE.

THAT'S JUST FINE.

I ONLY WISH THEY'D DO IT *FASTER*.

I DRAW THE SMOKE INTO MY LUNGS, EXTRACT THE NICOTINE AND THE TAR. IT DOESN'T DO ANYTHING FOR ME, BUT I LIKE THE SMOKE.

I LIKE THE *ASH*. THE WAY IT *FALLS*. I LIKE BREATHING OUT THE SMOKE.

I LIKE SMOKING CIGARETTES. IT'S SOMETHING NORMAL PEOPLE DO.

I SMOKE A CIGARETTE, AND PRETEND I'M NORMAL.

AND I WISH I WAS DEAD.

IT'S 10:20. MULLIGAN *MUST* BE IN BY NOW.

HELLO? EXTENSION 3440, PLEASE.

3440. *MULLIGAN?* IT'S ME. BLACKWELL.

OH. HELLO, RAINIE. WHAT'S NEW? YOU BEEN OUT RECENTLY?

UH. NO.

MULLIGAN, I'M *REALLY* DEPRESSED.

I'M SORRY TO HEAR THAT, RAINIE.

YESTERDAY, I JUST STARTED CRYING. AND I COULDN'T *STOP*. AND I JUST CRIED AND CRIED AND CRIED.

UM.

I'M *SORRY* TO LAY THIS ALL ON YOU, MULLIGAN. BUT YOU'RE THE *ONLY* PERSON I'VE GOT.

NO PROBLEM, RAINIE.

IS MY *CHECK* ON THE WAY THIS MONTH, MULLIGAN? I *THINK* IT MUST BE *LATE*. IT'S THE ONLY MAIL I GET, EXCEPT FOR JUNK MAIL. *YOU* KNOW.

YOUR CHECK DOESN'T GO OUT TILL THE LAST WEDNESDAY IN THE MONTH, RAINIE. YOU SHOULD KNOW THAT BY *NOW*.

I, UM. I SUPPOSE I FORGOT.

MULLIGAN? WHAT DO YOU *LOOK* LIKE?

HUH? I DUNNO, RAINIE. SORT OF NORMAL, I GUESS. BROWN HAIR. BROWN EYES. FIVE FOOT TEN. HOW ABOUT YOU?

YOU'VE *SEEN* THE *PHOTOS*, HAVEN'T YOU? IN MY *FILE?*

...YES.

I LOOK LIKE THEM.

YOU *WERE* REALLY CUTE. I MEAN *BEFORE*. FROM YOUR FILE.

I *CAN* LOOK LIKE THAT *NOW*, MULLIGAN. I CAN EVEN *FEEL* LIKE FLESH, SO YOU ALMOST COULDN'T TELL. *HONEST*.

MAYBE WE COULD MEET UP SOME TIME--

NOT A GOOD IDEA, RAINIE. YOU KNOW COMPANY POLICY.

2

90

YEAH. I KNOW THE COMPANY.

I GOTTA GET BACK TO WORK, RAINIE. YOU'RE NOT THE *ONLY* VET I GOTTA DEAL WITH. AND I'M PROCESSING CHECKS THIS AFTERNOON.

OH. TALK TO YOU NEXT WEEK, MULLIGAN.

BYE, RAINIE.

I SHOULDN'T HAVE PHONED HIM. NOW I CAN'T PHONE HIM FOR ANOTHER *WEEK.* I OUGHT TO HAVE *WAITED.* PUT IT OFF UNTIL AFTER LUNCH. MAYBE HE'D HAVE TALKED TO ME *LONGER*, AFTER LUNCH.

I WONDER WHAT HE LOOKS LIKE.

I WONDER WHAT MY FILE *SAYS* ABOUT ME?

MAYBE I COULD GO *UP* THERE SOME NIGHT AND...

WHAT IF THEY *CAUGHT* ME? THEY'D GET *MAD.* THEY'D *KNOW* IT WAS ME. THEY'D CUT MY DISABILITY PENSION. JUST *CUT* IT LIKE *THAT.*

AND THEN *NO ONE* WOULD TALK TO ME.

THE COMPANY. THE COMPANY IS ALL I'VE *GOT.*

AND *MULLIGAN'S* ALL I'VE GOT LEFT OF THE COMPANY.

NOBODY EVER COMES HERE. NOBODY PHONES.

NOBODY CARES ANY MORE.

DRIING DRIING

DRIING

THE PHONE

OH GOD.

PUT ON A BRAVE FACE.

IT'S JUST A TELEPHONE.

FAÇADE

DRIING

NEIL GAIMAN, writer   COLLEEN DORAN, penciller
MALCOLM JONES III, inker   STEVE OLIFF, colorist
TODD KLEIN, letterer   TOM PEYER, asst. editor
KAREN BERGER, editor

Featuring characters created by Neil Gaiman, Sam
Kieth and Mike Dringenberg.

ELEMENT GIRL created by
Bob Haney & Ramona Fradon

H-HELLO?

IS URANIA BLACKWELL THERE?

YES. YES, *THIS* IS SHE. *WH-WHO* IS THIS?

RAINIE? THIS IS *DELLA. DELLA KARIAKIS.* BUT I WAS DELLA *POTTER* WHEN YOU KNEW ME.

DELLA? I HAVEN'T SEEN YOU SINCE... *WHEN?* FIVE YEARS AGO?

NOT SINCE THE CRYPTOGRAPHY COURSE IN OREGON. I GOT YOUR PHONE NUMBER FROM *TRIANGLE.* HE DUG IT OUT OF ARCHIVES FOR ME.

TRIANGLE? HE'S STILL IN THE *COMPANY?* ARE *YOU?* STILL ACTIVE, I MEAN?

SURE. I, UH, HEAR YOU'VE *LEFT.*

SORT OF. PENSIONED OUT. SOME *PHYSICAL* STUFF.

YOU KNOW HOW IT IS.

YEAH. *LISTEN,* RAINIE, COULD I *SEE* YOU? FOR *LUNCH* OR SOMETHING? IF YOU'RE NOT *DOING* ANYTHING?

I... *I'M* NOT DOING ANYTHING.

GREAT. HOW ABOUT NEXT *TUESDAY.* IN THE *DA VINCI.* YOU KNOW-- THE ITALIAN PLACE IN THE MALL.

I... I CAN FIND IT.

GREAT. I'LL SEE YOU *THERE,* THEN. CIAO.

AND I SIT HERE. AND I LIGHT ANOTHER CIGARETTE, AND I TRY TO STOP TREMBLING.

I'LL HAVE TO PUT MY *FACE* ON.

5

93

I *HATE* MAKING FACES. THEY GIVE ME *DREAMS*.

I ONLY HAVE *TWO* KINDS OF DREAMS: THE *BAD* AND THE *TERRIBLE*.

BAD DREAMS I CAN *COPE* WITH. THEY'RE JUST NIGHT-MARES, AND THEY *END* EVENTUALLY.

I WAKE UP.

THE *TERRIBLE* DREAMS ARE THE *GOOD* DREAMS.

IN MY TERRIBLE DREAMS, EVERY-THING'S *FINE*. I'M *STILL* WITH THE *COMPANY*. I *STILL* LOOK LIKE *ME*. *NONE* OF THE LAST FIVE YEARS *EVER* HAPPENED.

SOMETIMES I'M *MARRIED*. ONCE I EVEN HAD *KIDS*. I EVEN KNEW THEIR *NAMES*. EVERYTHING'S *WONDERFUL* AND *NORMAL* AND *FINE*.

AND THEN I WAKE UP. AND I'M STILL ME.

AND I'M STILL HERE.

AND THAT IS *TRULY* TERRIBLE.

AND *THIS* DREAM?

RAINIE, IN *THAT* TOMB'S THE DOOHICKEY THAT TURNED REX MASON INTO A SUPER-MAN.

YOU'RE GOING IN THERE A *TOP* COMPANY OFFICER. BUT YOU'RE GOING TO COME *OUT* AN AMERICAN *SUPER-WOMAN*. FOR UNCLE SAM.

I NEVER *HAD* ANY UNCLES, TRIANGLE. *DID* I?

IN MY DREAM THE TOMB DOESN'T SMELL OF ANYTHING.

THE LAST TIME I CAME DOWN HERE IT SMELLED OF DUST, AND OF DEATH.

THAT'S THE *ORB OF RA.*

COME TO ME, DAUGHTER.

I AM RA. I AM THE SUN, WHO IS LIFE. I AM HE WHO IS BORN A CHILD EVERY MORN, AND DIES, AN OLD MAN, AT NIGHTFALL.

FROM MY SENILE SPITTLE AND FROM THE DUST, HUMANKIND WAS CREATED TO WALK THE EARTH, AND TO WORSHIP THE GODS.

6

YOU'D THINK, IF YOU CAN TURN YOURSELF INTO ANYTHING, THE EASIEST THING IN THE *WORLD* WOULD BE TO TRANSMUTE YOURSELF INTO *FLESH*. RIGHT?

NO.

I TRIED IT ONCE. NEVER AGAIN.

I COULDN'T GET RID OF THE *SMELL* FOR WEEKS.

ROTTEN MEAT.

SILICATE FACES ARE EASIER TO MANAGE. OKAY, IT HARDENS EVENTUALLY, AND FALLS OFF AFTER A DAY OR SO.

BUT AT *LEAST* IT DOESN'T *ROT*.

AND YOU CAN USE THE EMPTY FACES, FOR USEFUL THINGS.

THINGS NORMAL PEOPLE HAVE.

FAKING REAL HAIR IS EASIER. MOSTLY I USE METALS.

IT LOOKS *FINE* AS LONG AS NOBODY *TOUCHES* IT.

NOBODY EVER DOES.

EVERYTHING ELSE, YOU JUST COVER UP.

YOU CAN COVER UP SO *MUCH*.

OKAY, RAINIE. TIME TO FACE THE WORLD.

I FEEL *SICK*.

⑧

RAINIE? URANIA BLACKWELL? IS THAT *YOU?*

...*DELLA?*

YOU LOOK *INCREDIBLE*, HON! YOU HAVEN'T AGED A SINGLE *DAY!* YOU *MUST* TELL ME YOUR *SECRET.*

UH. *HI,* DELLA. IS THERE AN ASHTRAY?

I'M AFRAID THIS IS A NON-SMOKING RESTAURANT, MA'AM.

OH.

RAINIE. AREN'T YOU GOING TO TAKE OFF YOUR *GLOVES?*

NO!

I'VE GOT A *SKIN DISEASE.* IT'S WHY I HAD TO LEAVE THE COMPANY.

IT'S *LIKE* A SKIN DISEASE.

TAGLIATELLE VERDI, AND A GREEN SALAD. YOGURT DRESSING.

UH. SPAGHETTI *BOLOGNESE. PLEASE.*

...SURE. I'M STILL A COMPANY OFFICER. I'M IN *SIGNALS.* WHAT ARE *YOU* DOING THESE DAYS?

NOTHING.

NOTHING AT ALL.

9

THE REASON I WANTED TO TALK TO YOU IS THAT YOU'RE A *FRIEND*, RAINIE. AND YOU *AREN'T* COMPANY.

THERE'S *NO ONE* IN *CIA* I CAN *TALK* TO. IT-- IT'S NOTHING *BAD*.

IT'S JUST THAT I'M *PREGNANT*.

THE *FATHER*-- WELL, WE'RE *REALLY* IN *LOVE*, BUT HE'S IN ANOTHER DEPARTMENT. CO-INTEL-PROP. AND HE'S *STILL* MARRIED.

HE'S *GOING* TO GET A *DIVORCE*. BUT WE'VE *GOT* TO KEEP THIS *QUIET* UNTIL THEN.

BUT IF I DIDN'T TELL *SOMEONE* I'D BURST. JUST EX*PLODE*. AND YOU'RE MY OLDEST FRIEND, AND YOU'RE NOT *STRICTLY* COMPANY ANY MORE, BUT...

I'M SO *WORRIED*, RAINIE. YOU MUST *PROMISE* YOU WON'T TELL *ANYONE*.

I... I HARDLY EVER TALK TO ANYONE. I WON'T TELL ANYBODY.

OH *GOD*! RAINIE-- LOOK AT *THEM*! NOW, *THAT'S* SOMETHING THAT FREAKS ME OUT.

I'M *THIRTY-SIX*, AND THIS IS MY FIRST *BABY*. WHAT IF IT'S LIKE *THEM*?

WHAT IF MY *BABY'S* A *FREAK*?

THEY'RE JUST PEOPLE, DELLA. THEY *AREN'T* FREAKS.

IT'S *NOT* THAT I'VE GOT ANYTHING *AGAINST* THEM. IT'S JUST THAT THEY MAKE MY *SKIN CRAWL*.

10

SO, I DUNNO. WHAT DO *YOU* THINK I SHOULD DO, RAINIE? I MEAN--

RAINIE? WHAT'S WRONG WITH YOUR FACE?

RAINIE?

I--I'M SORRY, DELLA.

I'M SO SORRY.

MA'AM? ...UH, IS YOUR FRIEND ALL RIGHT?

SKIN DISEASE.

SHE'S GOT A SKIN DISEASE.

11

MY KEYS. MY KEYS ARE IN MY PURSE.

I MUST HAVE LEFT MY PURSE IN THE RESTAURANT.

5J

I CAN'T GO BACK THERE. I CAN'T.

MAGNESIUM.

I CAN'T DEAL WITH THIS.

I...

MULLIGAN. MULLIGAN WILL KNOW WHAT TO DO.

5J

EXTENSION 3440. P-PLEASE.

12

3440? MULLIGAN, PLEASE.

SORRY, MA'AM. MISTER MULLIGAN HAS BEEN TRANSFERRED TO ANOTHER DEPARTMENT.

NO! HE HAS TO BE THERE! HE MUST BE THERE!

TELL HIM IT'S ME. URANIA BLACKWELL. PLEASE. I HAVE TO TALK TO HIM. PLEASE? LOOK, JUST--

SORRY, MA'AM. OFFICER MULLIGAN IS NO LONGER HERE. CAN ANYBODY ELSE HELP YOU?

NO...

BUT THANK YOU.

WHAT AM I STILL WEARING THIS SHIT FOR?

NITROGEN.

I'M TALKING TO MYSELF. I THINK I'M CRACKING UP.

I THINK I CRACKED UP A LONG TIME AGO.

13

UM.
HELLO.

DO YOU
WANT TO *TALK*
ABOUT IT?

15

WHO ARE *YOU*? HOW DID YOU GET *IN*?

THE DOOR WAS OPEN. I HEARD YOU CRYING.

I'M *SORRY* IF I DISTURBED YOU.

YOU JUST LOOKED LIKE YOU MIGHT NEED SOMEONE TO *TALK* TO.

I... MAYBE I DO.

I'M SORRY. CIGARETTE?

NOT FOR ME.

NICE ASHTRAY.

IT--IT'S *NOT* AN ASHTRAY. I MEAN IT *IS*.

BUT IT'S *ALSO* MY *FACE*.

YOU SEE. SOMETIMES I HAVE TO LOOK *NORMAL*, AND THEN I GROW *FACES*.

BUT THEY DRY UP, AND FALL OFF, BUT I *COULDN'T* THROW THEM AWAY. THEY'RE *PART* OF ME.

SO I HANG ON TO THEM.

I... I'M PROBABLY NOT MAKING MUCH SENSE.

18

NO. YOU'RE MAKING SENSE.

YOU PEOPLE *ALWAYS* HOLD ONTO OLD IDENTITIES, OLD FACES AND MASKS, LONG AFTER THEY'VE SERVED THEIR PURPOSE.

BUT YOU'VE *GOT* TO LEARN TO THROW THINGS AWAY EVENTUALLY.

OHHHH.

HH. AAH. HHOOAH. UHH.

HEY? IT'S OKAY... I'M *SORRY.*

LOOK, I'VE GOT A *KLEENEX* SOMEWHERE. HERE YOU GO.

OHHM. HH. SNF. HH.

WHAT DID I SAY?

IT--IT'S JUHJUST WHUWHAT YUHYOU SUHSAID A--ABOUT *THROWING THINGS AWAY...*

I WANT TO DIE. I WANT TO KUH-*KILL* MYSELF.

AND-- AND I *CAN'T!*

IT'S NOT THAT I'M TOO *SCARED* TO KILL MYSELF.

I--I'M SCARED OF *LOTS* OF THINGS.

I'M SCARED OF *NOISES* IN THE *NIGHT-TIME,* SCARED OF *TELEPHONES* AND *CLOSED DOORS,* SCARED OF *PEOPLE...* SCARED OF *EVERYTHING.*

NOT OF DEATH.

I WANT TO DIE.

IT'S JUST THAT I DON'T KNOW *HOW.*

17

I'VE BEEN THINKING ABOUT IT FOR *SO* LONG, NOW. I CAN'T SLASH MY *WRISTS*--I DON'T HAVE ANY *BLOOD.*

WHEN I WAS AT HIGH SCHOOL, A KID SHUT HIMSELF IN A GARAGE, TOOK SLEEPING PILLS, CLIMBED IN THE CAR AND TURNED THE IGNITION.

"I *CAN'T* DO *THAT.* CARBON MONOXIDE'S JUST ANOTHER GAS, TO ME.

"AND MY BODY JUST *PROCESSES* POISONS."

I CAN'T *SHOOT* MYSELF. A BULLET WOULDN'T DO ANY *REAL* DAMAGE.

SO THEN I GET MORE EXTREME.

"MAYBE I COULD SIT AT *GROUND ZERO* OF A NUCLEAR TEST-- IF I COULD *FIND* ONE.

"BUT I'M *AFRAID* I COULD *SURVIVE* THAT. I *THINK* I WOULD.

"PERHAPS I'D BE RADIOACTIVE FOR ALWAYS...BUT I'D *SURVIVE.*"

THEN NO ONE WOULD *EVER* WANT TO TALK TO ME...

"I THOUGHT ABOUT TRANS-MUTING MYSELF TO FREE OXYGEN RADICALS AND JUST MELDING WITH THE *AIR.* OR WITH ADDED HYDROGEN, I COULD BECOME *WATER* AND JOIN MYSELF WITH THE SEA.

"BUT I'D PROBABLY *STILL* BE *CONSCIOUS.* JUST *SPREAD* OUT ALL OVER THE *WORLD.*"

I WANT IT TO *STOP.*

I DON'T *KNOW* HOW TO *STOP* IT.

HOW DID THAT *SONG* GO? FROM THAT TV SHOW?

SUICIDE IS ♪ PAINLESS ...IT ♪ BRINGS ON MANY CHANGES...AND ♪ I CAN TAKE OR ♪ LEAVE IT...

ISN'T IT *DUMB?* ALL OVER THE WORLD, PEOPLE RUNNING AROUND, TRYING *NOT* TO DIE?

HANGING ON TO LIFE LIKE GRIM DEATH.

AND I *WANT* TO DIE. AND I *CAN'T.*

18

IT'S NOT *THAT* BAD, RAINIE. EVEN THE METAMORPHAE DIE EVENTUALLY-- HEY, LISTEN, EVENTUALLY *EVERYTHING* DIES.

IT JUST TAKES A *LITTLE* BIT LONGER FOR YOU GUYS. BUT SOONER OR LATER YOUR MORPHOGENIC FIELD COLLAPSES--

--THE *METAPLASM* DISSOLVES, AND YOU'RE READY TO MOVE ON.

REMEMBER *ALGON?*

"HE WAS THAT ROMAN CENTURION--A METAMORPH, LIKE YOU. HE WAS *ONLY* 2,000 YEARS OLD, AND *HE* DIED."

"IN A *VOLCANO.* REMEMBER?"

BUT--HOW DO YOU *KNOW* THAT? THERE WAS *NOBODY* THERE. ONLY *REX* AND ME. NO ONE ELSE.

ME.

...WHO *ARE* YOU?

DON'T YOU *KNOW?*

YES. I THINK I DO.

AND YOU'VE *COME* FOR *ME?* BLESSED, MERCIFUL DEATH. YOU'VE COME TO MAKE IT ALL *STOP?*

19

NO. I HAVEN'T COME FOR YOU, RAINIE.

THERE WAS A WOMAN UPSTAIRS, CHANGING THE LIGHT BULB IN HER KID'S ROOM. THE STEPLADDER *SLIPPED*...

LIKE I SAID: I WAS *PASSING* AND I HEARD YOU *CRYING*, AND, WELL, THE DOOR *WAS OPEN*...

ANYWAY: I'M *NOT BLESSED, OR MERCIFUL.* I'M JUST *ME*. I'VE GOT A *JOB* TO DO, AND I *DO* IT.

LISTEN: EVEN AS WE'RE TALKING, I'M THERE FOR OLD AND YOUNG, INNOCENT AND GUILTY, THOSE WHO DIE TOGETHER AND THOSE WHO DIE ALONE.

I'M IN CARS AND BOATS AND PLANES; IN HOSPITALS AND FORESTS AND ABATTOIRS.

FOR SOME FOLKS DEATH IS A *RELEASE*, AND FOR OTHERS DEATH IS AN *ABOMINATION*, A *TERRIBLE THING.*

BUT IN THE *END*, I'M THERE FOR *ALL* OF THEM.

RAINIE, IN WEST AFRICA A SMALL VILLAGE IS BEING MASSACRED BY MERCENARIES, IN PAY OF THEIR OWN GOVERNMENT. I'M *THERE*.

IN THE FARTHEST REACHES OF A DISTANT GALAXY, A PLANET IS BEING RIPPED APART BY INTERNAL STRESSES; THE PLANET WAS THE HOME OF MANY CRYSTAL INTELLIGENCES, CALM AND FINE AND BEAUTIFUL. I AM *THERE* AS WELL.

I'M IN *ALL* THOSE PLACES, AND I'M ALSO HERE, TALKING TO YOU.

BUT... I'M *NOT* YOUR DEATH.

AT LEAST, NOT *YET*.

WHEN THE FIRST LIVING THING EXISTED, I WAS THERE, WAITING.

WHEN THE LAST LIVING THING DIES, MY JOB WILL BE *FINISHED*.

I'LL PUT THE *CHAIRS* ON THE *TABLES*, TURN OUT THE *LIGHTS* AND *LOCK* THE *UNIVERSE* BEHIND ME WHEN I *LEAVE*.

I--I DON'T THINK I *UNDERSTOOD* ALL THAT.

BUT--ARE YOU SAYING YOU *WON'T* HELP ME? IS *THAT* WHAT YOU'RE SAYING? THAT I'VE GOT ANOTHER *TWO THOUSAND YEARS* OF BEING A *FREAK*?

TWO THOUSAND YEARS OF *HELL*?

YOU MAKE YOUR **OWN** HELL, RAINIE.

OKAY. I'LL HELP YOU. IF THAT'S WHAT YOU **WANT.**

THAT'S WHAT **I** GET FOR GETTING **INVOLVED.**

YOU'LL **KILL** ME? TAKE MY **LIFE?** GIVE ME **OBLIVION?**

YOUR LIFE IS YOUR OWN, RAINIE. **SO** IS YOUR DEATH.

AND **OBLIVION...?** THAT'S **NOT** AN OPTION, I'M AFRAID.

HMM. RAINIE, MYTHOLOGIES TAKE LONGER TO DIE THAN PEOPLE BELIEVE. THEY LINGER ON IN A KIND OF DREAM COUNTRY THAT AFFECTS ALL OF YOU.

WHAT DO YOU KNOW ABOUT **RA?**

HE WAS A SUN GOD. IN ANCIENT EGYPT.

YEAH. THAT'S RIGHT.

HE'S SEEN **BETTER** DAYS. HE **STILL** KEEPS BRINGING THE METAMORPHAE INTO EXISTENCE, EVEN THOUGH THE BATTLE YOUR KIND FOUGHT FINISHED **AGES** AGO.

IT'S HIS **NEVER-ENDING BATTLE** AGAINST APEP, THE SERPENT THAT NEVER DIES.

DUMB. I **TOLD** HIM, "THE SERPENT THAT NEVER DIES IS **DEAD.** I TOOK HER **THREE THOUSAND YEARS AGO!** THE NEVER-ENDING BATTLE **ENDED...**"

IF YOU **REALLY** WANT TO END THIS LIFE, RAINIE, YOU OUGHT TO TALK TO **HIM.**

21

TALK TO HIM? BUT HE'S IN *EGYPT*. I *CAN'T GO TO* EGYPT. I...

OH, *HONESTLY*. IT'S LIKE TALKING TO A *WALL*...

SORRY, RAINIE, BUT YOU PEOPLE ARE SO *SLOW*. LOOK.

THE *ORB OF RA*. IT'S NOT *ONLY* IN A *TOMB*...

HE'S A *SUN GOD*, RAINIE.

HE'S THE *SUN*. WELL, SORT OF. ONE OF THEM.

HE'S OUT THERE RIGHT NOW, RAINIE. *SEE?* TALK TO HIM BEFORE HE SETS.

BUT ASK POLITELY.

WHAT DO I *SAY?*

JUST TALK TO HIM. SAY WHAT YOU FEEL.

UM. *RA?*

HELLO? *RA?*

HE *SPOKE* TO ME. DID YOU *HEAR* THAT? HE ACTUALLY *SPOKE* TO ME!

PLEASE, SIR--I DON'T *WANT* TO BE ME. THANK YOU FOR MAKING ME SPECIAL, BUT I DON'T *WANT* TO BE SPECIAL.

I JUST WANT IT TO *STOP*.

CAN YOU MAKE ME *NORMAL* AGAIN?

PLEASE?

LOOK AT YOU? YOU WANT ME TO *LOOK* AT YOU?

BUT YOU *MUSTN'T*. YOU MUSTN'T *LOOK* AT THE *SUN*...

WELL. OKAY.

22

HAVE FUN, RAINIE.

BETTER LUCK NEXT TIME.

DRIING DRIING

HI.

YOU WANT RAINIE? SHE'S GONE AWAY, I'M AFRAID.

WHERE IS SHE *NOW?* I WOULDN'T LIKE TO SAY FOR CERTAIN.

NO. SHE'S *NOT* LIVING HERE ANY LONGER.

NO, MISTER MULLIGAN. I REALLY *CAN'T* GET A MESSAGE TO HER. I'M *SORRY.*

WHO AM *I?* JUST A *FRIEND.* SOMETIMES. MAYBE.

SORRY I COULDN'T HELP ANY.

BE SEEING YOU...

FELIX'S HOUSE. RIC IS NO

LESSLY IN FRONT OF HIM —

BLANKLY. HE'S RAISED HIS

DS OF THE FINGERS ARE RE

THEY'RE ALMOST JUST NU

FELIX HAS REACHED DOW

SUSPECT HE'S STANDING UP

S PROBABLY JUST HIS ONE

ANY MORE.

at did you do to your hands'

SCRIPT INTRODUCTION
by NEIL GAIMAN

Then I stripped them, scalp from
skull, and my hunting dogs fed full
And their teeth I threaded neatly
on a thong;
And I wiped my mouth and said,
"It is well that they are dead,
"For I know my work is right and
theirs were wrong."

But my Totem saw the shame;
from his ridgepole-shrine he came,
And he told me in a vision of the night:—
"There are nine and sixty ways of
constructing tribal lays,
"And every single one of them is right!"

Rudyard Kipling.
IN THE NEOLITHIC AGE. 1895

It took a little time before I could be persuaded to allow a script to be published.

For the same reason that a magician doesn't want to let you backstage when he rehearses, for the same reason you should never wander around a film set: it spoils the magic when you know how it's done.

But we all have a craving to see behind the illusion. We want to know how the magician managed to saw the lady in half without spilling blood, and put her together afterwards, apparently unharmed; we want to wander the studio back-lots and stare at the backless houses. And some of us want to know how a comic gets written.

I did.

I have always wanted to write comics. (That's not strictly true: I have always wanted to *write*, to tell stories. Comics were and are one of the media I wanted to tell stories with.)

But I could never figure it out; *how* did a writer get the story in his head onto a comics page? What did a comics script look like? What did a comics writer do?

I eventually found out, by asking someone who wrote comics (it was Alan Moore—one of the best writers ever to work in this medium) and getting him to show me what a script looked like, and how it was laid out. This he did, on one side of notebook paper.

Once I knew what a comics script looked like, the rest was easy. (No, that's not true. The rest was pretty difficult; and every story presents its own set of problems. But you know what I mean.)

Which is why I eventually agreed to allow this script to be printed. I've even added some marginal notations, and dug out from my files the folded, stapled mini-comic for this issue. (I always make a small doodled version of the comic while I'm writing, to let me know how many panels I'm putting on a page, and to suggest ideas of layout and storytelling.)

Let me throw in a warning before you begin to read the script.

This is only how *I* write a comics script. Specifically how I write SANDMAN.

There are thousands of people out in the world writing comics, and none of the others write scripts quite like this. Some just write a sequence of panel descriptions, not worrying how they'll fall on the page. Some draw doodles of what they want for an artist, with the dialogue in the margins. Sometimes the writers just suggest a plot, and then come back to it at lettering stage and write the dialogue then. Sometimes they write something closer to a movie script, just dialogue and action, and let the artists break down the story into panels.

These are all valid ways of writing a comics script. I've used a few of them myself. (But not for SANDMAN.)

A few writers put in much more detail than you'll see in this script. Some writers use far less. Some writers don't know or care who'll be drawing the story they're writing. Some do. (I do). Some artists write and draw (and often letter and colour) their own comics, and they have different ways again of writing scripts for themselves.

Which means, I suppose, that this *is* a typical comics script, insofar as every script is atypical. And it's the way I write SANDMAN.

(All the other ways of writing scripts are right, too. That's what the quotation at the top of the page is about.)

Each SANDMAN script is a letter to the artist (I drive Karen Berger, my long-suffering editor, crazy, by refusing to write a script unless I know who's going to draw it; if you write for an artist you can play to their strengths. It makes you look good); and this is a letter to Kelley Jones. (It was the first time we'd ever worked together; and working with Kelley has been fun. He's a terrific artist and a nice person.)

We picked this script to 'Calliope' for this book as probably the most interesting for a casual reader the script for 'A Midsummer Night's Dream' is longer and technically far more complex (it was much the hardest of these scripts to write), but it's also probably a lot less interesting simply to read, or so I have been assured.

To reiterate: this isn't How To Write Comics The Neil Gaiman Way. It's a script for 'Calliope.' It's being printed here to satisfy your curiosity (if you have any) about what a SANDMAN script looks like.

There are a number of talented people involved in the production of SANDMAN. In this issue, after Kelley pencilled it, Todd Klein lettered the comic, then Malcolm Jones inked it, going over Kelley's pencils in black ink, getting the artwork to a point at which it could be reproduced (and incidentally adding a great deal to the look of the book), Robbie Busch coloured it, and somewhere in the background Karen Berger and Tom Peyer knocked themselves out making sure that everything made sense, got from place to place on time, and that we all got paid.

If you've read 'Calliope' already, you know the story. Now you're going to see the script.

You don't have to read it, if you don't want to.

But for those of you who do, welcome backstage.

Let us show you how it was done...

Neil Gaiman

Episode 17

HI KELLEY,

WELCOME TO THE WEIRD WORLD OF SANDMAN. WHAT WE'RE DOING IS A
SERIES OF SHORT STORIES FOR FOUR OR FIVE ISSUES HERE; I'VE FINISHED THE
DOLL'S HOUSE STORYLINE, AND THERE WAS A WHILE TOWARD THE END OF
THE STORYLINE WHEN I JUST COULDN'T TAKE IT ANY MORE -- PARTLY
BECAUSE I'D KEEP GETTING NEW IDEAS FOR STORIES AND BE UNABLE TO GET
THEM IN, AND ALSO BECAUSE I WANTED TO DO A FEW TOTALLY SELF-
CONTAINED STORIES THAT I COULD GET OVER WITH IN 24 PAGES: THE WORRY
THAT I DIDN'T HAVE A CLUE HOW DOLL'S HOUSE WAS GOING TO END (WHICH I
DIDN'T, UNTIL I GOT THROUGH SANDMAN 15) WAS GETTING PRETTY NERVE-
WRACKING...

THIS IS THE FIRST OF THEM. I'M CALLING THE SHORT STORIES "DREAM
COUNTRY." INCIDENTALLY, KELLEY, I WRITE PRETTY FULL SCRIPT, FOR THE
MOST PART. HAVING SAID THAT, IT'S A GUIDE: IF YOU SEE A WAY TO IMPROVE
IT, MAKE IT WORK BETTER, THEN GO FOR IT. YOU'RE THE ARTIST, AFTER ALL.

OK -- LET'S GO.

THEY SAY THAT ON AMERICAN COP SHOWS A LOT.
....

ODD FACTS AND COINCIDENCES DEPT: SO FAR THE SANDMANS I'VE STARTED
AND THEN HAD TO RESTART, BECAUSE THEY WERE HEADING OFF IN THE
WRONG DIRECTION WERE: 2,7,12 AND NOW THIS ONE, 17. EVERY FIVE ISSUES...
....

OKAY KELLEY -- THE BAD NEWS. THE REASON WHY THIS IS PROBABLY GOING
TO BE SLIGHTLY LATE IS ALSO THE REASON THAT IT BEARS NO RESEMBLANCE
TO THE STORY I TOLD YOU ON THE PHONE. THIS IS BECAUSE I STARTED THE
ONE I TOLD YOU ABOUT, SEX AND VIOLETS, TWICE, GOT SEVEN PAGES INTO ONE
VERSION AND TEN PAGES, THE SECOND TIME, ON A TOTALLY DIFFERENT
TREATMENT, AND EACH TIME IT DIED ON THE PAGE. WHICH MEANT THAT I
BASICALLY HAD TO DECIDE WHETHER TO TRY AGAIN, OR TO STRIP THE STORY
DOWN AS FAR AS I COULD, TAKE WHAT I COULD, AND START AGAIN. I SUSPECT
AT SOME POINT I'LL COME BACK TO OLD PUCK, BUT IN THE MEANTIME WE'VE
GOT A DIFFERENT STORY ABOUT A DIFFERENT MUSE, AND ABOUT THE TWO
MEN WHO HAVE HELD HER IN THRALL, AND ABOUT THE SANDMAN, AND HIS
REVENGE ON THEM. IT'S A DARKER STORY THAN THE OTHER, CREEPIER AND
LESS COMFORTING.

THE GOOD NEWS IS THAT I'M 99% SURE IT'LL WORK THIS TIME, AND I HOPE
YOU ENJOY DRAWING IT AS MUCH YOU WOULD HAVE THE OTHER.

.....

EDITORS NOTE: The script comments that appear on the following pages,
in red and blue ink, are by Neil Gaiman and Kelley Jones, respectively.

Calliope.

Page 1 panel 1

WE ARE LOOKING AT THE FACE OF RICK MADOC. NO PANEL BORDER --
HE'S IN CLOSE UP, FULL FACE, LOOKING AT SOMETHING BELOW HIM
WITH AN EXPRESSION OF INTERESTED DISTASTE. HE'S THIN, MID-
THIRTIES, RED SHORT-CUT HAIR. NOT A CLASSICAL COMIC BOOK FACE --
HE'S GOOD-LOOKING IN A JOHN LENNONISH SORT OF WAY.

Caption - top right: May 1986.

Madoc:I don't have any idea.

Madoc:So what is it? It smells quite disgusting.

Page 1 panel 2

PULL BACK. WE'RE IN A ROOM IN MADOC'S HOUSE: HIS STUDY,
BOOKSHELVES ON THE WALLS, A DESK WITH A WORD PROCESSOR ON
IT. A SET OF ENCYCLOPEDIAS. FAIRLY MODERN. MAYBE SOME
PAINTINGS ON THE WALL. LITTLE STATUES HERE AND THERE. THERE'S
A SLIM TELEPHONE ON A TABLE IN ONE CORNER, AND, IN THE
OPPOSITE CORNER OF THE ROOM, A DOOR TO THE WORLD OUTSIDE. BUT
THAT'S ALL BACKGROUND, AND WE DON'T NEED TO PUSH IT HERE --
DROP IT IN AS WE MOVE AROUND THE ROOM, LOOKING AT THESE
PEOPLE. WE'RE LOOKING AT MADOC, WHO IS WEARING A BROWN
LEATHER JACKET, TEE SHIRT AND JEANS, AND A YOUNGER MAN, IN
GLASSES, A DOCTOR (ALTHOUGH NOT WEARING A WHITE COAT) FELIX
GARRISON. DR GARRISON IS HOLDING SOMETHING OUT -- IT'S BLACK,
LIKE A LARGE, HAIRY STONE, OR A FOSSILISED TRIBBLE COVERED IN
SLIME. IT'S A TRICHINOBEZOAR -- YOU MAY BE ABLE TO FIND A
REFERENCE PICTURE OF SOME KIND IN A MEDICAL DICTIONARY. THE
DR LOOKS RATHER PLEASED WITH HIMSELF. IT'S EARLY EVENING IN
EARLY SUMMER OR LATE SPRING.

Garrison:It's what you were asking for. It's a bezoar.

Madoc:Hang on, I thought they were like, precious stones?

Page 1 panel 3

WE'RE LOOKING AT THE GUNKY, HORRIBLE, CALCIFIED MASS, HELD IN
THE DOCTOR'S HAND, IN CLOSE UP. IT LOOKS REVOLTING. MAKE IT
LOOK HAIRY AND SLIMY AT THE SAME TIME: IMAGINE A CAT-SICKED-
UP HAIRBALL TO THE MAX...

DR:Most of them are.

This is a trichinobezoar -- it's made of hair. I cut it out of a young
woman's stomach this afternoon. Lovely long hair she had. Trouble was,
she'd been sucking it, chewing it, -- swallowing the hairs.
Must've been doing it for years.

[Handwritten margin note:] Guy Lawley M.D. found me a photo of a trichobezoar afterwards. It looked a lot like what Kelley had drawn. Guy is the only doctor I know who also writes comics from time to time, and he hears my stranger requests, for obscure cancers or diseases, with more respect than they perhaps deserve.

Page 1 panel 4

PULL BACK AGAIN. WE CAN SEE, CLOSE TO US, THE DR, LEANING DOWN, OR
CROUCHING, GETTING A BOOK OUT OF HIS LARGE BLACK DOCTOR'S BAG. HE'S
LEFT THE THING ON THE TABLE, AND RICK IS STARING AT IT IN DISGUST.
POSSIBLY POKING AT IT WITH A FINGER.

Dr:Technically that's known as the Rapunzel syndrome.
Anyway, it's a bezoar. Mission accomplished.

Madoc:It's disgusting. But thanks. What do I owe you, Felix?

Page 1 panel 5

OKAY -- WE'RE LOOKING AT THE TWO OF THEM. FELIX IS HOLDING OUT A
BOOK TOWARDS RICK, A LITTLE NERVOUSLY. RICK'S JUST PLEASED NOT TO
HAVE TO HAVE PAID ANY MONEY FOR THIS THING. IF WE CAN SEE THE BOOK --
IT'S A HARDBACK, BY THE WAY -- IT'S CALLED THE CABARET OF DR CALIGARI,
BY RICHARD MADOC.

Dr:Oh, nothing.

It would have only been incinerated, or popped into a jar for students to stare at.
Just don't tell anyone where you got it.

And, um, I was wondering if you'd sign this for me?

Rick:Sure. No problem.

Page 2 panel 1

WE ARE LOOKING AT THE TITLE PAGE OF THE BOOK -- WE CAN SEE PRINTED OR
TYPESET, IN BLACK, THE CABARET OF DR CALIGARI, RICK'S NAME, AND
UNDERNEATH THAT, IN BLUE OVERLAY LETTERING, HANDWRITING -- POSSIBLY
WE CAN SEE A PEN AT THE BOTTOM FINISHING OFF THE SIGNATURE. KELLEY,
UNLESS YOU WANT TO DRAW ANY HANDS HERE, OR THE PEN, THIS IS
PROBABLY ALL TODD'S PANEL.

TODD CAN DO IT, MY PENMANSHIP SUCKS. K

Book title -- black printing: The Cabaret of Dr Caligari.
By Richard Madoc.

Handwriting -- blue overlay:For Felix Garrison, with thanks, Rick Madoc.

Rick: (off): There you go.

Page 2 panel 2

FELIX, HOLDING THE BOOK AT ARMS' LENGTH, IN BOTH HANDS, READING THE
INSCRIPTION. HE LOOKS REALLY PLEASED.
Felix:This is great. It's a real thrill for me, to, you know, be able to do something
for one of my heroes. I loved the book. Amazing stuff.

Felix:So, um, what do you need the bezoar for?

Page 2 panel 3

WE'RE LOOKING AT RICK. HE SEEMS SLIGHTLY UNCOMFORTABLE AT THIS.

Rick:Like you were asking the other day -- where do writers get our crazy ideas?
Heh.

Rick:It's research, really.

Felix:I heard you were writing a sequel to the Cabaret -- I'm really excited.

Rick:Oh. Great.

Page 2 panel 4

FOREGROUND -- THE PHONE. IN THE BACKGROUND WE CAN SEE RICK, HEADING
FOR THE PHONE, AND FELIX, PICKING UP HIS BAG, AND PREPARING TO LEAVE.

Rick:Uh, that's the phone. Listen, thanks again for the thing.

Felix:No problem. I know how busy you are. I'll just let myself out, then. 'Bye.

FX: Near phone, small: Breep breep.

Page 2 panel 5

KEEP THE PHONE IN THE SAME POSITION IT WAS BEFORE, BUT RICK IS NOW IN
THE FOREGROUND, AND HE'S PICKED UP THE PHONE. IS TALKING INTO IT.
POSSIBLY WE CAN SEE FELIX GOING OUT THE DOOR INTO THE STREET, OR
POSSIBLY HE SIMPLY ISN'T IN THE ROOM ANY LONGER.

Rick:Hello? Richard Madoc speaking.

Phone:Rick? It's Harry. Listen, we have to talk. Your publishers were onto me
again today.

Rick:Oh. Hi Harry.

Page 2 panel 6

SIMILAR SHOT, ONLY RICK LOOKS REALLY MISERABLE, UNCOMFORTABLE,
SHIFTY. AS IF HE DOESN'T WANT THIS CONVERSATION.

Phone:Listen, the novel's almost nine months overdue, and they're threatening to
cause trouble. You're in breach of contract, Rick.

Phone:Is it finished yet?

Rick:Nearly finished.

Phone:Well, how much have you got to go?

Page 2 panel 7

SIMILAR SHOT, ONLY WE'VE GRADUALLY CLOSED IN ON RICK. HE
LOOKS LIKE HE'S LYING.

Rick:It's almost finished, Harry. You can't rush these things. Another
couple of weeks, maybe, okay?

Listen, I'm really busy. I'll get back to you.

Rick:Okay?

Page 3 panel 1

THREE PANELS ON THE TOP TIER. PULL BACK, SO WE'RE LOOKING AT
THE WHOLE OFFICE. RICK'S PUT THE PHONE DOWN. HE'S LOOKING AT
IT, WITH HIS ARMS FOLDED.

Rick:How much of the novel have I written? Honestly?

Page 3 panel 2

HE'S PICKING UP THE BEZOAR, THE HAIRBALL, CAREFULLY, AND
DISTASTEFULLY, AND IS DROPPING IT INTO A PLASTIC SHOPPING BAG.

Rick:Nothing.

Page 3 panel 3

RICK'S GOING OUT THE DOOR, CARRYING THE SHOPPING BAG. HE
LOOKS SLUMPED, LESS HYPER.

Rick:Not a word.

Page 3 panel 4

WE'RE OUTSIDE FOR THE FIRST TIME. LONG PANEL ACROSS THE
MIDDLE OF THE PAGE. IT'S SUNSET, AND THE SKY IS LIT WITH A MESS
OF REDS AND ORANGES. RICK MADOC IS WALKING DOWN A LONDON
STREET, HIS BACK TO US, CARRYING THE PLASTIC SHOPPING BAG. I'LL
GET YOU PHOTOREFERENCE ON THE KIND OF STREETS WE'RE LOOKING
AT HERE: CHELSEA-ISH AREA, WHICH PROBABLY MEANS NOTHING TO
YOU, BUT YEARS AGO WHEN I WAS A CHILD, IT WAS WHERE THE
PUNKS STARTED UP, ON THE KING'S ROAD, AND I ONCE HAD A
GIRLFRIEND WHO LIVED OVER A BANK JUST OFF THE KING'S ROAD. I
MERELY TELL YOU THIS TO ADD ATMOSPHERE TO AN OTHERWISE DRY
AND UNEXCITING PANEL DESCRIPTION. THE STREET IS PRETTY MUCH
DESERTED. I DOUBT WE CAN SILHOUETTE HIM AGAINST THE SKYLINE,
UNLESS HE'S ACTUALLY WALKING BESIDE THE THAMES HERE --
ANYWAY, I'LL TAKE A PILE OF PHOTOS AND YOU CAN TAKE YOUR PICK

I spent a fun afternoon wandering around chelsea and photographing Embankment reference

WHERE YOU PUT HIM. MAKE IT MOODY, THOUGH. LONG, EXPRESSIONIST
SHADOWS. THE STREET SHOULD BE DIRTY, NEWSPAPER BLOWING DOWN IT.

No dialogue.

Page 3 panel 5

BOTTOM TIER -- THREE PANELS. HE'S STANDING IN A DOORWAY, PRESSING THE
ENTRYPHONE BUTTON: THERE'S ONLY ONE BUTTON, AND WE CAN ASSUME
THAT WHOEVER OWNS THIS PLACE, A TERRACED RED-BRICK GOTHIC
MONSTROSITY JUST LIKE ALL THE OTHERS ON THE STREET, LIVES THERE
ALONE. ALL THE OTHERS WERE TURNED INTO APARTMENTS THIRTY YEARS
EARLIER AND FORTY PEOPLE LIVE WHERE FIVE DID IN THE EARLIER YEARS OF
THE CENTURY.
Entryphone: (jagged or square)Who is it?

Rick:Richard Madoc, to see Erasmus Fry.

Entryphone:I'll be straight down.

Page 3 panel 6

SAME SORT OF SHOT. SHIFT AROUND SLIGHTLY, SO WE'RE LOOKING HEAD ON
TO THE DOOR, AND RICK HAS HIS BACK TO US. THE DOOR HAS BEEN OPENED
ABOUT AN INCH, AND WE CAN SEE AN OLD EYE STARING OUT OF THE
DARKNESS AT US. ACTUALLY, TO GET THIS TO WORK, I THINK WE'LL HAVE TO
COME IN FOR A CLOSE-UP. WE CAN SEE THE CHAIN ON THE DOOR IS STILL IN
PLACE.

Erasmus:Are you alone?

Rick:Yes. It's just me. I've got it.

Erasmus:Well, come in, dear boy. Come in.

Page 3 panel 7

THE DOOR IS COMPLETELY OPEN NOW. AN ELDERLY MAN IS STANDING THERE,
LOOKING A LITTLE NERVOUS. HIS NAME IS ERASMUS FRY. REALLY IT IS. HE'S
WEARING A TARTAN CHECK DRESSING GOWN, AND TROUSERS AND CARPET
SLIPPERS. HE'S GOT AN OLD-FASHIONED WHITE SHIRT ON, NOT TUCKED INTO
HIS TROUSERS, AND A DUSTING OF WHITE STUBBLE ON HIS CHIN, OF THE KIND
THAT INDICATES THAT HE CAN'T BE BOTHERED TO SHAVE. HE'S GOT A SHOCK
OF WHITE HAIR, AND AN OLD FACE THAT'S STILL STRONG; LIKE AN ELDERLY
SHERLOCK HOLMES. HE'S A FAMOUS NOVELIST AND PLAYWRIGHT, OR HE WAS,
THIRTY YEARS AGO.   *PURE BRIDE of FRANKENSTEIN*

Erasmus:I'm not sorry that I'm not dressed for visitors. When you get to my age,
you don't give a toss what you look like. Heh.

Erasmus:Don't just stand there. Come in.

Page 4 panel 1

NOW, WE'RE IN ERASMUS FRY'S HOUSE FOR THE NEXT FOUR PAGES, AND IT'S
CLAUSTROPHOBIC AND CRAMPED -- LONG, DIMLY LIT CORRIDORS, CRAMMED
WITH OLD STATUARY AND PHOTOGRAPHS AND BOOKS. BLACK PANEL BORDERS
TO BLEED FROM HERE UNTIL THE END OF PAGE SEVEN. THREE PANELS ON THE
TOP TIER. THEY'RE IN THE HALLWAY. IT'S DARK AND GLOOMY, WITH LARGE
OLD PHOTOGRAPHS HANGING ON THE WALLS. THE OLD MAN IS SHUFFLING
DOWN THE CORRIDOR WITH THE YOUNGER MAN, TALLER, BEHIND HIM. THE
HALLWAY IS ALSO SET WITH MIRRORS, REFLECTING THE FACES OF THE MEN.
ERASMUS IS NOT A NICE OLD MAN.

Erasmus:How are you, M'boy? Written anything profound and stirring recently?

Rick:You know I haven't, Mister Fry.

Erasmus:No. We'll go into my study, and you can show me my present.

page 4 panel 2

THEY'RE NOW IN THE OLD MAN'S STUDY. THE OLD MAN IS STANDING UP AND
POURING TWO GLASSES OF SHERRY FROM A CUT-GLASS DECANTER. WHEN WE
SEE IT, THE STUDY IS EXPENSIVELY FURNISHED, DOMINATED BY A LARGE
BLACK- AND -WHITE PHOTOGRAPH OF ERASMUS AGED ABOUT TWENTY. EMPTY
FIREPLACE. IT'S ALL DUSTY. IT LOOKS LIKE IT HASN'T BEEN CLEANED OR
TIDIED FOR YEARS. THERE ARE A COUPLE OF ARMCHAIRS IN THERE, AND A
DESK. RICK IS ABOUT TO SIT IN AN ARMCHAIR. HE'S STILL HOLDING THE
PLASTIC BAG.

Erasmus:Ah -- an excuse for a sherry.

Erasmus:Cheap stuff, of course. I'm not wasting the good stuff on a little shit like
you.

Page 4 panel 3

ERASMUS, SITTING IN THE ARMCHAIR, RAISING THE GLASS OF SHERRY TO HIS
LIPS. HE'S ABOUT TO GIVE A LECTURE TO RICK. HE'S PROBABLY RAISING ONE
FINGER, OR LEANING HIS CHIN ON ONE HAND. HE'S NOT SMILING. HE LOOKS
VERY COMFORTABLE.

Erasmus: Let me tell you about Bezoars. Word comes from the Persian. Pad-zahr.
It means counter-poison. Antidote. Mainly found in the stomachs of goats and
gazelles.

— DESCRIPTION IN PARACELSUS BOOK

Page 4 panel 4
AGAIN, RUN THIS ACROSS THE MIDDLE OF THE PAGE. THE TWO OF THEM
SITTING IN ARMCHAIRS, OPPOSITE EACH OTHER: THE YOUNG MAN, ANTSY,
SCARED, NERVOUS; THE OLD MAN, COMFORTABLE, POWERFUL. RICK HAS PUT
HIS SHERRY DOWN ON THE FLOOR, ISN'T DRINKING IT. WE CAN SEE
BOOKSHELVES ACROSS THE WAY -- POSSIBLY A CHESS SET IN ONE CORNER.
THEY'RE IN THE LOWER HALF OF THE PANEL, LEAVING PLENTY OF ROOM FOR
THE HUGE WORD BALLOONS.

Erasmus:Once believed to possess mystic powers: they can remedy poison, make the sick well. Edward IV survived the effects of a poisoned wound, due solely to a bezoar in his possession.

Queen Elizabeth the First had a bezoar set in gold, with unicorn's horn, given to her by John Dee, her spy and magician.

Page 4 panel 5

THREE PANELS ON THE BOTTOM TIER. WE'RE LOOKING AT RICK -- HE'S SITTING THERE LISTENING TO THIS STUFF, GETTING MORE AND MORE IRRITATED -- HE'S PROBABLY LOOKING UPWARDS, BORED AND NERVOUS. NEARLY EXASPERATED. THE BACK OF THE ARMCHAIR FRAMES HIS HEAD.

Erasmus (off):For the common people, apothecaries would lend out bezoars at extortionate rates, for a week, or a fortnight...

Page 4 panel 6

SAME SHOT, BUT RICK'S HALF-STOOD UP, PUSHING HIMSELF UP WITH HIS ARMS AT HIS SIDE. HE LOOKS UPSET, IRRITATED, ANGRY.

Rick:Will you shut up?

I haven't written a word in a year -- nothing I haven't thrown away! Do you know what that's like?

Rick:When it's just you, and a blank sheet of paper?

Page 4 panel 7

MOVE IN ON RICK. HIS FACE IS SHADOWY, AND PAINED. IT'S LIKE HE'S BARING HIS SOUL HERE.

Rick:When you can't think of a single thing worth saying, a single character that people could believe in, a single story that hasn't been told a thousand times before...

Page 5 panel 1

THE OLD MAN HAS STOOD UP, IS LOOKING DOWN SHARPLY. HE'S REACHING OUT HIS HAND.

Erasmus:Of course I know what it's like. Don't be a fool, boy.

Erasmus:Let me see my present.

Page 5 panel 2

THE OLD MAN HOLDING UP THE BEZOAR, ADMIRING IT ON HIS OPEN HAND. HE'S IN LECTURE MODE AGAIN.

Erasmus:Oh yes. Rapunzel, let down your hairball. A genuine trichinobezoar. The smell comes from the partly digested particles of food, trapped in--

Erasmus:I'm sorry. I'm lecturing again. An old writer with no-one else to talk to gets fond of the sound of his own voice...

Page 5 panel 3

ERASMUS AND RICK ARE BOTH STANDING UP, NOW. ERASMUS HAS EXTENDED AN ARM, IS USHERING RICK OUT OF THE ROOM.

Erasmus:I will put the bezoar with the rest of them.

I suppose that you want her, now.

Did you bring any clothes?

Rick:Clothes? I didn't know I...

Erasmus:Never mind. I have an old coat you may use.

Page 5 panel 4

THEY'RE WALKING UP STAIRS, NOW, A NARROW, DARK STAIRWAY, HUNG WITH BOOK-COVERS AND PLAYBILLS, ALL WITH THE NAME ERASMUS FRY ON THEM, IN LARGE LETTERS. I DON'T KNOW IF WE CAN SEE ANY TITLES IN THIS OR THE NEXT PANELS, BUT THEY'RE THINGS LIKE A STRANGER IN EDEN OR HALL OF SHADOWS OR HERE COMES A CANDLE, THINGS THAT SOUND LIKE FAMOUS NOVELS OF THIRTY YEARS AGO. RICK IS NERVOUS, ERASMUS KNOWS EXACTLY WHERE HE'S GOING.

Erasmus:I caught her on Mount Helicon, you know. 1927. Greece. I was 27. I'll be 87 next year.

She was bathing in a spring, and I caught her and bound her with Moly -- sorcerer's garlic, as it's sometimes called -- and with certain rituals.

Page 5 panel 5

THEY'RE AT THE TOP OF THE STAIRS, WALKING DOWN A NARROW CORRIDOR. IF YOU WANT TO MESS WITH THE ANGLES, SO THE INSIDE SEEMS SUBTLY WRONG, THEN BE MY GUEST. IT'S REALLY DARK. WE OUGHT TO BE ABLE TO SEE THEM, BUT IT'S VERY GLOOMY AND ILL-LIT, ERASMUS HAS PULLED OUT A KEY, WHICH HE'S HOLDING IN FRONT OF HIM. I SUSPECT THEY'RE WALKING TOWARDS US. ERASMUS IS IN THE FRONT, OF COURSE.

Erasmus:The hardest part was getting her back to England.

Erasmus:They say one ought to woo her kind, but I must say I found force most efficacious...

After all, I got the fame and the glory. I created the novels, the poems, the plays...

Page 5 panel 6

THEY'RE STANDING IN FRONT OF A DOOR. ERASMUS HAS PUT THE KEY
INTO THE LOCK, AND IS TURNING THE KEY. ONE BARE BULB DANGLES
FROM A FRAYED FLEX, LIGHTING THE HALLWAY, JUST. I MEAN, IT'S
ABOUT A FIFTEEN WATT BULB, BUT IT'S A BULB.

Erasmus:I don't need her anymore, Madoc. And you do.

Here she is.

AND THEN WE GO OVER THE PAGE TO SEE WHAT'S IN THE ROOM...

PAGE 6 PANEL 1

SPLASH PAGE. DARK BORDER AROUND THE PAGE. WE'RE LOOKING
STRAIGHT THROUGH THE OPEN DOOR -- POSSIBLY THE PANEL BORDER
IS THE DOORWAY. AND WE'RE LOOKING AT IS APPARENTLY A THIN,
FIFTEEN-YEAR OR POSSIBLY JUST-SIXTEEN OLD GIRL. SHE'S STANDING
THERE STARING AT US. SHE HAS A BEAUTIFUL FACE, WITH DEEP
CHEEKBONES -- SHE'S A GODDESS AFTER ALL -- AND A THIN BODY: SHE
LOOKS AS IF SHE'S BEEN STARVED FOR A COUPLE OF WEEKS. WE CAN
SEE THE OUTLINE OF HER HIPBONES, AND NOT QUITE COUNT HER RIBS.
SHE'S NAKED. SHE LOOKS VERY VULNERABLE -- THIS IS THE
VULNERABILITY OF NAKEDNESS; IF YOU'VE EVER SEEN ANY PHOTOS
OF FAMINE VICTIMS, OR CONCENTRATION CAMP VICTIMS, THERE'S A
POINT AT WHICH NAKEDNESS TOTALLY CEASES TO TITILLATE, INSTEAD
JUST AROUSES FEELINGS OF PITY. (BILL SIENKIEWICZ CAUGHT IT
PERFECTLY IN THE MENTAL HOSPITAL SEQUENCES IN ELEKTRA:
ASSASSIN #1.) EITHER SHE HAS HER HANDS ON HER OPPOSITE
SHOULDERS, HUGGING HERSELF, OR SHE'S COVERING HER BREASTS
WITH ONE ARM, AND REACHING DOWN WITH HER OTHER HAND,
COVERING HER PUBIC AREA WITH A HAND. IT'S NOT FALSE MODESTY --
IT'S A WISH TO PROTECT HERSELF FROM. SHE DOESN'T LOOK SCARED --
NERVOUS, PERHAPS, OR UNHAPPY MORE LIKE. SHE ALSO HAS MASSES
OF SHAGGY BLONDISH HAIR, DOWN TO THE SMALL OF HER BACK. THE
KEY HERE IS VULNERABILITY -- THIS SHOULDN'T LOOK TITILLATING,
IT'S NOT A HUBBA HUBBA KIND OF NAKED WOMAN SHOT; IT'S ONE
THAT IT ALMOST HURTS TO LOOK AT. TEAR THEIR HEARTS OUT,
KELLEY. SHE'S LIT BY THE MUTED BULB IN THE HALL. DIMLY BEHIND
HER WE MIGHT BE ABLE TO MAKE OUT A CHEAP CAMP BED WITH A
THIN BLANKET ON IT. AT THE BOTTOM OF THE PANEL, PREFERABLY IN
THE KIND OF LETTERING WE HAD FOR THE TITLE OF #7, IS THE TITLE.

Erasmus (off, left): Her name's Calliope.

Title: Calliope.

And Credits.
At the bottom of the page, Sandman (logo) characters created by Gaiman,
Kieth and Dringenberg.

Kelley drew Calliope as really really skinny, with horribly protruding ribs. Karen felt that this was too extreme, and when Malcolm inked it he made her a little less skinny...

Page 7 panel 1

(JUST A BRIEF APOLOGY -- I'M AFRAID ERASMUS TALKS AN AWFUL LOT, AND
MAKES SURE HE TAKES THE LONGEST POSSIBLE ROUTE THROUGH ANY
SENTENCE. I TRY TO KEEP HIM SHORT-WINDED, BUT HE DOES RATHER TEND TO
OVERLOAD ANY PANELS HE'S IN WITH WORDS. OH WELL --AT LEAST THIS IS HIS
LAST PAGE ON STAGE, AS IT WERE... IF NECESSARY YOU COULD SLIP THIS
PANEL ONTO THE BOTTOM RIGHT HAND CORNER OF THE SPLASH PAGE, BUT I
THINK IT'LL WORK BETTER AS A SPLASH.) WE'RE LOOKING AT CALLIOPE, IN
CLOSE UP. A FACE SHOT, SHADOWY, AS SHE STARES STRAIGHT OUT AT US.
SHE'S COME OUT OF THE ROOM, AND IS NOW IN THE HALLWAY, SO THE LIGHT
IS DIRECTLY ABOVE HER, CASTING LOW SHADOWS FROM HER NOSE AND
ACROSS HER EYES. I TEND TO IMAGINE HER AS A STARVED YOUNG BRIGITTE
BARDOT, BUT THAT'S POSSIBLY BECAUSE THERE'S A BRIGITTE BARDOT MOVIE
ON LATE NIGHT TV RIGHT NOW. SHE HAS A COMBINATION OF GRANDEUR AND
INNOCENCE, HERE, BUT OBVIOUSLY HATES ERASMUS, IS COUNTING THE DAYS
AND THE HOURS UNTIL HER IMPRISONMENT IS OVER. HE MAY HAVE HER
SPIRIT, BUT HE DOESN'T HAVE HER SOUL, AND SHE SAYS:

Calliope:What would you with me now, Erasmus? Am I now to perform for your
amusement? Is this man to be our audience?

Page 7 panel 2

ANOTHER FULL-PANEL FACE SHOT, HEAD AND SHOULDERS, THIS TIME OF
ERASMUS, PROBABLY NOT LOOKING DIRECTLY AT US, BUT OFF SLIGHTLY. HE'S
BITCHY AND OLD AND HATES EVERYTHING, ESPECIALLY HER.

Erasmus:Don't get yourself all worked up, Calliope.

No, this is Richard Madoc. He's a novelist -- or at least, he's written one extremely
successful first novel, and has found himself quite unable to write anything else.

Page 7 panel 3

NOW WE'RE LOOKING AT RICK, AGAIN FULL FACE, AS HE STARES AT US, LIPS
PRESSED CLOSE TOGETHER, STARING AT THE GIRL (AT US) HIS EXPRESSION
UNREADABLE. MAKE THESE THREE PANELS VERY SIMILAR, JUST WITH
DIFFERENT PEOPLE IN THEM, IF YOU SEE WHAT I MEAN.

Erasmus (off):Richard, this is Calliope. The youngest of the nine muses. She was
Homer's muse, so she ought to be good enough for you.

Calliope, I'm giving you to Richard. You're his now.

Page 7 panel 4

PULL BACK NOW. CLOSE TO US, ON THE RIGHT OF PANEL, HER BACK TO US, IS
CALLIOPE, AND BEYOND HER, FACING US, ARE THE OLD MAN, AND, TALLER
AND YOUNGER AND ILL-AT-EASE, MADOC. HER ARMS ARE NOW AT HER SIDES.

Calliope:But you said -- you told me, you promised that you would free me before
you died. You said I could have my freedom...

Erasmus:Put not your trust in princes, my dear.

Page 7 panel 5

BACK TO CALLIOPE. SHE'S CRYING, SILENTLY. ONE TEAR IS
TRICKLING DOWN HER FACE. SHE'S RAISED A HAND TO HER
MOUTH, BUT HER CHIN IS STILL RAISED PROUDLY.

Erasmus (off):Nor in an aging author who has never been what one
might call a shining example when it came to keeping his word...

Writers are liars, my dear. Surely you have realised that by now?

Page 7 panel 6

PULL BACK AGAIN FOR A LONG SHOT. MADOC IS PUTTING A COAT
AROUND CALLIOPE'S SHOULDERS. ERASMUS HAS TURNED HIS BACK
ON BOTH OF THEM, IS WALKING TOWARDS US.

Erasmus:Take the little cow away, Madoc. I never want to see either
of you again.

Page 7 panel 7

OUT ON THE STREET, NOW. MADOC AND CALLIOPE ARE STANDING
THERE -- SHE'S WEARING THE COAT, BUTTONED UP, AND NOTHING
UNDER IT, SO WE CAN SEE HER BARE LEGS AND FEET ON THE
HARD SIDEWALK. ERASMUS IS STANDING IN THE DOORWAY,
FACING THEM, FACING US. FOR THE ONLY TIME, HE LOOKS
VULNERABLE, INSECURE. HE LOOKS OLD.

Erasmus:However, if you ever happen to feel a spark of gratitude,
you might want to persuade some publisher to bring 'Here Comes A
Candle' back into print.

Erasmus:I was particularly proud of that one.

Page 8 panel 1

THIS IS OPPOSITE AN AD PAGE. OKAY. NOW, FOR THE FIRST TIME
WE SLIDE OUT OF REAL-TIME AND INTO AN ALMOST MONTAGE
MODE. OVER THE NEXT FEW PAGES WE'RE GOING TO COVER A FEW
YEARS IN REAL TIME. WE'RE ALSO OPENING UP HERE, SO THE
FEELING OF CLAUSTROPHOBIA, WE SHOULD HAVE GOT FROM THE
LAST FEW PAGES, SINCE WE ENTERED FRY'S HOUSE, SHOULD BE
RELIEVED. WHITE PANEL BORDERS HERE AGAIN, FOR THE FIRST
TIME SINCE PAGE 4. WE'RE LOOKING AT THE TOP, ATTIC ROOM OF
A HOUSE -- MADOC'S HOUSE, -- FROM OUTSIDE. WE CAN SEE THE
BRICKWORK, AND A WINDOW, BARRED WITH A METAL GRILLE.
THROUGH THE WINDOW WE CAN SEE, ON THE INSIDE, CALLIOPE,
LOOKING AT US SILENTLY. SHE'S NAKED AGAIN, BUT WE CAN
PROBABLY ONLY SEE HER HEAD AND BARE SHOULDERS, AND THE
SIDE OF HER ARMS.

Caption:And Madoc took Calliope back to his home, and locked her in
the topmost room, which he had prepared for her.

*WHITE INK ON BLACK
FOR FIGURE of CALLIOPE*

-12-

Page 8 panel 2

NOW I WANT TO TRY TO GET ACROSS THE RAPE, AND THE HORROR *(obvious reasons)*
AND THE DOMINANCE, FAIRLY SUBTLY, DOING ALL THE WORK IN
THE READER'S HEAD. THE WHOLE THING SHOULD BE REALLY
UNDERSTATED. WHAT WE'RE ACTUALLY LOOKING AT IN THIS PAGE
ARE BARE WOODEN FLOORBOARDS. AND COMING IN FROM THE
RIGHT, WE CAN SEE CALLIOPE'S LEFT ARM AND HAND, PALM
UPWARD, LAYING FLAT ON THE FLOOR. COMING DOWN FROM
ABOVE IS RICK'S RIGHT ARM; HIS HAND IS CLAMPED AROUND HER
WRIST, HOLDING IT DOWN TO THE GROUND. THAT'S ALL WE CAN
SEE.

Caption:His first action was to rape her, nervously, on the ~~bare
wooden floor~~. musty old camp-bed.

Caption:She's not even human, he told himself. She's thousands of
years old. But her flesh was warm, and her breath was sweet, and
she choked back tears like a child whenever he hurt her.

Page 8 panel 3

WE ARE NOW DOWN IN HIS STUDY, FROM PAGE ONE, AND HE'S
SITTING DOWN IN THE CHAIR NEXT TO HIS WORD-PROCESSOR,
SMOKING A CIGARETTE. HE LOOKS VERY PLEASED WITH HIMSELF,
SMILING A LAZY SMILE, HIS FEET UP ON THE DESK. THE SMOKE
FROM THE CIGARETTE DRIFTS UPWARD. HE'S NOW BAREFOOT, AND
JUST WEARING JEANS AND A SINGLET.

Caption:It occurred to him momentarily that the old man might have
cheated him: given him a real girl. That he, Rick Madoc, might
possibly have done something wrong, even criminal...

Caption:But afterwards, relaxing in his study, something shifted
inside his head.

Page 8 panel 4

WE'RE NOW BEHIND THE WORD PROCESSOR. WE CAN SEE THE
BACK OF HIS HEAD, PERHAPS HIS HANDS ON THE KEYBOARD. AND
WE CAN SEE THE SCREEN, IN FRONT OF HIM. I'LL GIVE YOU SOME
TEXT THAT COULD BE REDUCED AND PUT ON THE SCREEN --
FAILING THAT JUST MAKE IT CLEAR THAT THERE'S TEXT ON THE
SCREEN. ANOTHER POSSIBILITY IS THAT WE CAN SEE HIS FACE
REFLECTED IN THE SCREEN, OR PARTLY REFLECTED ON ONE SIDE
OF THE SCREEN. IF WE CAN, HE'S SMILING.

Screen: CHAPTER THREE. "AND SOME IN VELVET GOWNS"

"Your face," he said to her. "What have you done to your face?"

Marion shrugged. "I wanted to look on the outside like I do on the
inside," she said simply, not putting down the knife.

Caption:He switched on the word processor to write it down before it fled.

Caption:He had been writing for three hours before he surfaced enough to realise that he had begun his second novel.

Although they aren't together in this collection, the ad placement in the original comic should have ensured that pages 9 and 10 were opposite each other the [in] Sandman #17 in the...

Page 9 panel 1

OKAY, FIVE PANELS ON THE PAGE, IN THREE TIERS. TOP TIER OF THREE PANELS, THEN TWO PANELS BELOW THAT. BASICALLY IT'S A NINE-PANEL GRID. FIRST PANEL, WE'RE LOOKING AT CALLIOPE, SITTING ON THE FLOOR OF THE ATTIC ROOM, IN THE CORNER OF THE ROOM, HANDS CLASPED IN FRONT OF HER. SHE'S STILL SORT OF NAKED, BUT, ALONE, SHE'S MORE COMFORTABLE WITH HER NAKEDNESS: HAVING SAID THAT, BEAR IN MIND THAT THE MUSES (UNLIKE THE GRACES) WERE ALWAYS DEPICTED CLASSICALLY AS BEING DRESSED IN LIGHT SHIFTS: THEY WERE ALWAYS CLOTHED, SO SHE'S NOT AT EASE, NAKED. ACTUALLY, ON REFLECTION, HOW ABOUT KEEPING HER IN THE COAT THAT SHE WAS IN BEFORE, ALTHOUGH IT'S NOT ACTUALLY DONE UP: IT'S LOOSE AND OPEN, ALTHOUGH IT WOULD SHADOW HER BODY. WE'RE ABOUT FIVE FEET AWAY FROM HER.

Calliope:Gracious ladies, mother of the Camenae, hear my prayer.
Calliope: Melete, Mneme, Aiode, attend my supplication.

PLAY with Angles + LAYOUT - CONTRAST Calliope to emptiness of the Attic

Page 9 panel 2

RIGHT, WE'RE ZOOMING IN ON HER, SO NOW WE'RE LOOKING AT HER CHEST TO HEAD HERE. SHE'S LOOKING DOWN -- HER HANDS STILL CLASPED IN FRONT OF HER. SHE'S PRAYING, AND SHE'S ALSO VERY SAD, HURTING INSIDE. SHE HAS NO HOPE THAT ANYONE WILL RESPOND.

calliope:It is I, your daughter Calliope, who calls you, as I have called you a thousand times. I...

I implore you, ladies, deliver me from this place and this time.

Page 9 panel 3

RIGHT, WE'VE GOT A FINAL CLOSE-UP ON HER FACE, FRAMED BY THE FALLING HAIR, EYES LOOKING DOWN, OR HIDDEN BY LASHES.

Calliope:To whom can I speak, in my grief? I who am laden with wretchedness.

Calliope:Ladies of Meditation, Remembrance and Song, hearken to me.

The panel placement meant we moved a few of these balloons around.

Page 9 panel 4

OKAY -- THIS ONE RUNS ALL THE WAY ACROSS THE MIDDLE TIER: LEFT TO RIGHT, WE'RE LOOKING AT MELETE, MNEME, AIODE. NOW WE'RE PLAYING WITH A RUNNING THEME IN SANDMAN, OF THE TRIPLE GODDESS. HUNTING

THROUGH MATERIAL ON THE MUSES (NINE OF THEM -- THREE TIMES
THREE) I DISCOVERED THERE WAS AN EARLIER VERSION OF THE
MUSES WHEN THERE WERE ONLY THREE -- THIS THREE -- AND IT MADE
MORE SENSE THAT THEY'D COME FROM AN EARLIER, TRIPLE VERSION
OF THE MUSES THAN THAT, AS IN OTHER VERSIONS OF THE LEGENDS,
THEY WERE THE DAUGHTERS OF ZEUS AND MNEMOSYNE (MEMORY).
CHECK OUT SANDMAN 10 PAGE 19, AND THE DAVE MCKEAN COVER TO
SANDMAN 2: THIS IS THE VERY BASIC DESIGN FOR THE THREE, BUT
HAVING SAID THAT, FEEL FREE TO DESIGN YOUR OWN VERSIONS.
BASICALLY THEY ARE ALL WEARING WHITE CLASSICAL SHIFTS:
MELETE, THE OLD HAG ON THE LEFT, LOOKS LIKE A VERY OLD
WOMAN, HER STRAGGLY HAIR LONG AND GREASY, HER ARMS THIN
AND BONY; MNEME IS BASICALLY THE FACE FROM THE COVER OF
SANDMAN 2, RATHER THAN EITHER MIKE OR SAM'S VERSIONS OF THE
CHARACTER, BUT HER HAIR IS LONGER, AND WE CAN SEE HER FIGURE
THROUGH THE SHIFT -- IT'S HUGE BREASTS AND HUGE HIPS, AS WITH
ANY OLD STATUES OF THE EARTH MOTHER: HER ARMS ARE CROSSED
ACROSS HER HIPS, HER FACE ROUND AND MOTHERLY; AND ON THE
RIGHT STANDS AIODE, TALL AND HAUGHTY, WITH MASSES AND
MASSES OF BLONDE HAIR TUMBLING AROUND HER. THE CRONE, THE
MAIDEN, THE MOTHER. BEHIND THEM WE CAN EITHER SEE DARKNESS,
OR THE BARE WALLS OF THE ATTIC ROOM. THIS IS PROBABLY WAIST
TO HEAD SHOTS, AND A FOOT OR SO ABOVE THEIR HEADS. *OLD WOMAN WILL BE MY NEIGHBOR*

Melete:All right. Enough, Beautiful Voice. Why do you call us?

Mneme:We feel your pain, daughter, but we cannot help you.

Aiode:You were snared upon Helicon according to the mysteries. You are
lawfully bound.

Page 9 panel 5

SMALL INSET SQUARE PANEL ON THE RIGHT -- CALLIOPE'S FACE,
TALKING URGENTLY TO THE WOMEN.

Calliope:But it is not just, my mothers. I can bear this burden no more.

Is there nothing you can do? No-one who can intercede on my behalf?

Page 9 panel 6

LONG PANEL ACROSS THE BOTTOM OF THE PAGE. THE THREE AGAIN,
ALTHOUGH NOW THEY'VE CHANGED POSITION, THE OLDER AND THE
YOUNGER HAVE SWAPPED PLACES. AND WE'VE MOVED IN CLOSER TO
THEM. THE YOUNGER ONE LOOKS SYMPATHETIC, THE MIDDLE ONE
LOOKS MOTHERLY, THE OLDER ONE LOOKS UNSYMPATHETIC.

Aiode:There are few of the Old Powers willing or able to meddle in mortal
affairs in these days, Calliope.

Mneme:Many gods have died, my daughter; while aspects of other gods
have been lost for ever.

Melete:Hehh. Only the Endless will never die -- and even they are having a difficult
time of late.

Still, every little bit helps, as the old woman said when she pissed in the sea.

A genuine old English proverb, strangely enough.

Page 10 panel 1

THE WOMEN HAVE STARTED TO TALK AMONG THEMSELVES, HAVE TURNED
INWARDS -- LEFT TO RIGHT THE ORDER NOW GOES MOTHER, MAIDEN, CRONE,
BY THE WAY -- AND ARE DISCUSSING WHAT THEY CAN DO ABOUT THIS.

Mneme:The Endless -- now, there's a thought -- after all, the Dream-King and
Calliope were close, long ago. For a short while. Weren't you, my pet?

Aiode:Not for long. And, remember, sister-self, they did not part on the best of
terms.

Melete:But she did bear his cub.

That boy-child, who went to Hades for his lady-love, and died in Thrace, torn apart
by the sisters of the frenzy, for his sacrilege.
Page 10 panel 2

INSET PANEL, SMALL AND SQUARE, OF CALLIOPE'S FACE -- SHE LOOKS
HOPEFUL, AND DESPERATE. (NOTE, SHE NEVER APPEARS IN THE SAME PANEL
AS THE 3 SISTERS).

Calliope:Not him. Not after what he did to me. He hates me for that, and I despise
him. I would not accept his help.

Page 10 panel 3

PANEL ACROSS THE CENTRE TIER OF THE PAGE, CLOSE IN SO THAT WE'RE JUST
LOOKING AT THE THREE FACES OF THE WOMEN, STARING DOWN AT US (OLD
ONE, YOUNG ONE, MOTHER, LEFT TO RIGHT). BEAR IN MIND THAT THESE ARE
NOT WOMEN BUT ARCHETYPES -- IN THIS CASE A GRECIAN VARIANT ON THE
ONE-WHO-IS-THREE WE'VE SEEN BEFORE.

Melete:Foolish child. Oneiros is in no position to help you, even if he wished to --
which is unlikely, to put it mildly.

Aiode:You see, just like you, Calliope, your one-time admirer has been ensnared by
mortals.

And while you are imprisoned in your tower, he is immured beneath the ground.

Mneme:I am sorry, my little one. Your prayers were wasted. There is nothing we
can do for you, and nothing you can do but hope.

Page 10 panel 4

OKAY -- NOW WE GO BACK TO THREE PANELS ON THE BOTTOM TIER, LIKE THE
THREE PANELS ON THE TOP OF PAGE 9. (BEAR IN MIND THAT BECAUSE OF THE
AD PAGE ON PAGE 8 THESE TWO PAGES ARE OPPOSITE EACH OTHER,
ALTHOUGH DON'T MAKE THEM A DOUBLE PAGE SPREAD.) CALLIOPE'S STOOD

UP. WE'RE FAIRLY CLOSE UP ON HER STANDING FIGURE. SHE'S LOOKING
TOWARDS US, ARMS OUTSTRETCHED, PALMS UPWARD, PLEADING.

Calliope: No -- please, come back, please. There must be something, there must be
someone who can free me...

Page 10 panel 5

PULL BACK FROM CALLIOPE A LITTLE FURTHER. SHE'S LOWERING HER HANDS
TO HER SIDES. SHE'S TALKING TO AN EMPTY ROOM.

Calliope:Please... Send someone... anyone...

Page 10 panel 6

OKAY, PULL BACK ALL THE WAY. CALLIOPE IS A SMALL FIGURE, HER HANDS
BY HER SIDES; WHILE WE CAN SEE ALL THE ROOM AROUND HER, AND IT'S
TOTALLY EMPTY. THE THREE WOMEN HAVE GONE.
Calliope: (small) Even Oneiros.

Page 11

I DUNNO IT'S HALF PAST FIVE IN THE MORNING, AND THE TV IS SHOWING AN
"IN-DEPTH EXAMINATION" OF THE CLOSING OF A CANADIAN RAILROAD; AT
FOUR IN THE MORNING I WAS RUNG THREE TIMES IN SUCCESSION BY SOMEONE
OR SOMETHING WHO DIDN'T SPEAK. INITIALLY I THOUGHT IT WAS JUST
SOMEONE CALLING FROM THE U.S. WITH A BAD LINE, BUT THE THIRD TIME I
THOUGHT I HEAR RUSTLING AND BREATHING. SPOOKED THE SHIT OUT OF ME, I
CAN TELL YOU. ANYWAY, I WANTED TO GET THROUGH PAGE 12 TONIGHT, BUT
I'LL BE HAPPY IF I CAN GET TO THE END OF PAGE 11. *It WASN'T ME. K*

Page 11 panel 1

AT THE TOP LEFT OF THE PAGE IS CALLIOPE'S FACE, SHADOWY, INTENSE -- NOT
IN A PANEL BORDER. I SUSPECT WE'D ONLY ACTUALLY GET THE LEFT SIDE OF
HER FACE, IF SHE'S STARING STRAIGHT IN FRONT OF HER, AND GOING OFF
INTO A FLASHBACK, THE RIGHT HAND SIDE OF HER FACE WOULD MERGE WITH
THE PANEL WE'RE GOING INTO, IF YOU SEE WHAT I MEAN; SO THE LEFT SIDE
OF HER FACE, FRAMED BY HAIR, IS ALMOST PANEL BORDER. OH, WHILE I
THINK OF IT, ALTHOUGH SHE'S THIN, AND NOT 100% CLEAN, HER HAIR IS
STILL FAIRLY UNMATTED, SHE'S NOT ILL, OR ACTIVELY STARVING, OR
ANYTHING -- THIS IS BECAUSE SHE'S ONE OF THE IMMORTALS. PERHAPS SHE'S
LOOKING SLIGHTLY TO THE RIGHT.

Caption:It had been her own fault.

Caption:Spring 1927. Mount Helicon.

Caption:She had only returned for a brief time, lured perhaps by nostalgia...

Page 11 panel 2

OKAY -- SEGUE INTO THE PANEL FROM THE LAST ONE. WE'RE LOOKING
AT CALLIOPE AS SHE WAS OVER SIXTY YEARS AGO. SHE LOOKS NOW
LIKE A HAPPY FIFTEEN-YEAR-OLD BRIGITTE BARDOT. SHE'S WEARING
A WHITE CLASSICAL SHIFT, AND IS UP TO HER THIGHS IN WATER, ON A
GOLDEN, SUNNY DAY, IN GREECE. SHE LOOKS VERY YOUNG AND VERY
HAPPY. ONE IDEA MIGHT BE TO COLOUR THIS IN VERY VIVID COLOURS;
ANOTHER IDEA MIGHT BE TO DO THIS PANEL AND THE NEXT IN SEPIA --
POSSIBLY A BETTER IDEA, BECAUSE GETTING COLOURS TO APPEAR
MORE VIVID THAN THEY DO AUTOMATICALLY CAN BE A REAL BITCH.
ON THE BANK OF THE POOL IS A SCROLL.

Caption:She had laid down her scroll, and was bathing in a clear pool,
remembering the lost, golden days: when the nine were still sought and
wooed and needed...

Caption:When the music of the spheres still resonated [echoed] in mortal
souls.

Page 11 panel 3

DO THIS PANEL NEXT TO THE OTHER ONE, WITH ONLY A THIN WIGGLY
LINE BETWEEN THIS PANEL AND THE LAST. CALLIOPE'S VIEWPOINT.
WE'RE LOOKING AT A YOUNG, 27-YEAR-OLD ERASMUS FRY,
RECOGNISABLE FROM THE PHOTOS WE SAW IN HIS HOUSE, EARLIER.
HE'S WEARING A 1920S SUIT, NO HAT, HAS DARK, SLICKED-BACK
HAIR, AND IS STANDING FAIRLY CLOSE TO US (HE'S ON DRY LAND, BUT
WE'RE PROBABLY LOOKING AT HIM FROM WAIST TO HEAD), GRINNING
LIKE A WOLF. IN ONE HAND HE'S HOLDING LONG-STEMMED WILD
GARLIC FLOWERS, IN THE OTHER HE'S HOLDING A ROLLED-UP
PARCHMENT SCROLL, HOLDING IT TOWARDS US. HIS EYES ARE BRIGHT,
AND HE'S A TOTAL BASTARD.

Caption:In one hand he held Moly flowers, that had power over her kind,
and in his other hand he held her scroll.

Caption:Which one are you? He had asked her.

Caption:Calliope, she told him.

Caption:Kall-i-oh-pee, he had echoed, as if he were tasting her name.

Page 11 panel 4

ACROSS THE CENTRE OF THE PAGE IS THE SCROLL, LAID
HORIZONTALLY ACROSS -- NOT IN A PANEL BORDER: IT'S BURNING,
FLAMES LICKING UP FROM IT.

Caption:And then he smiled. Well, he said, you can call me master.

Caption:And then he burned her scroll.

Page 11 panel 5

BOTTOM TIER. THE ATTIC ROOM -- RICK HAS ENTERED. HE LOOKS REALLY
HAPPY. SHE'S STANDING THERE IN HER COAT, HER EXPRESSION SET. STARING
AT HIM. MEDIUM SHOT.

Madoc:Hey! Great news! I've finished the novel. It's called "And My Love She
Gave Me Light." Two drafts in five weeks. And it's all good stuff.

Calliope:I am pleased for you. Now will you let me go?

You can find the [ancient] riddle this line is taken from in Book Four of "The Books of Magic", at the end of time.

Page 11 panel 6

CLOSE IN ON THE TWO OF THEM CLOSE. HE'S PUTTING HIS ARMS AROUND HER.
SHE'S LOOKING UP AT HIM SADLY.

Madoc:Are you out of your mind? This is just the beginning. Come here, gorgeous.
Let's make two and a half minutes of squelching noises...
Calliope:Please, Madoc. Let me go. Stop forcing me to do these things.

Page 11 panel 7

LIKE PANEL ONE -- JUST MADOC'S FACE, LOOKING STRAIGHT AT US, NO PANEL
BORDER. IF YOU JUST DID THE LEFT SIDE OF CALLIOPE'S FACE AT THE TOP,
THEN JUST DO THE RIGHT SIDE OF MADOC'S FACE HERE, HIS FACE SET AND
HARD. IF HE'S SMILING, HE'S SMILING CRUELLY. IF SHE WAS LOOKING OFF TO
THE RIGHT IN THE FIRST PANEL, THEN HERE HE'S LOOKING SLIGHTLY OFF TO
THE LEFT.

Madoc:Listen. You're my possession, until I tell you that you're free. Don't
forget it.

 You're my personal muse, sweetheart. Now.

Let's party.   *SHOCKING - NOT SEXUAL*

Page 12

OKAY -- THIS PAGE AND THE NEXT ARE A SERIES OF QUICK HOPS, WATCHING
RICK MAKING IT UP TO THE TOP OF THE TREE. KEEP ALL THE PANEL BORDERS
HERE VERTICAL, AND KEEP THE PANELS DISTINCT FROM EACH OTHER. IT'S
BASICALLY A SIX-PANEL GRID -- THREE ON THE TOP TIER, THREE BELOW.

Page 12 panel 1

THE TOP HALF OF PAGE 12. WE'RE AT A PARTY -- IT'S A PUBLISHER'S PARTY,
WELL-LIT. PEOPLE ARE MILLING AROUND, SMALL KNOTS OF PEOPLE, SOME OF
THEM DRINKING GLASSES OF WINE. IN THE MIDDLE OF THE PARTY IS A
DISPLAY OF THE BOOK, WITH, ABOVE IT, A HUGE MOCK-UP, OF THE BOOK
COVER. IT'S CALLED "...AND MY LOVE SHE GAVE ME LIGHT," THE COVER
SHOWING A CANDLE BURNING ON A SKULL, AND, AT THE BOTTOM OF THIS, RIC
MADOC. (HE'S LOST THE K FROM HIS NAME, FOR REASONS OF COOL.) BIG

PHOTO OF HIM IN THE BACKGROUND. THERE COULD BE A FEW
BALLOONS AROUND, POSSIBLY WITH REPRODUCTIONS OF THE BOOK
COVER ON THEM. SOME OF THE PEOPLE -- MEN AND WOMEN -- ARE
REALLY WELL DRESSED, SOME ARE FASHIONABLY SLOPPY: SOME OF
THEM ARE LOOKING SIDELONG AT RICK -- HE'S THE STAR, AFTER ALL.
STANDING NEXT TO RICK, WHO'S ON THE EXTREME RIGHT, FAIRLY
NEAR TO THE BOOK DISPLAY, IS RICK. HE'S IN A GOOD SUIT, LOOKING
REASONABLY COMFORTABLE. HE'S GRINNING. NOW REMEMBER, HE'S
GOING TO GET BETTER DRESSED AND COOLER SLICKER OVER THE NEXT
PAGE OR SO, SO WE DON'T WANT TO BLOW IT ALL HERE. STANDING
NEXT TO HIM IS AN ATTRACTIVELY DRESSED YOUNG WOMAN WITH
LONG BLACK HAIR AND TOO MUCH MAKE-UP. HE'S SMOKING A
CIGARETTE. IT'S REALLY UP TO YOU HOW MANY PEOPLE YOU DRAW,
BUT TRY TO GIVE THE IMPRESSION THAT THIS A WELL-ATTENDED
LUNCH PARTY SOMEWHERE QUITE LARGE.

Caption:May 1987.

Boring psuedy type on the left (small):
Really, John, I don't see any way that a work of genre fiction could be
nominated for the Booker prize.

Another boring psuedy type next to him (small):
Well, I feel in the light of his latest novel that Madoc's work has to be
seen as transcending genre. It's as if it were written by a different man.

Someone: (small)It's a beautiful book. Quite remarkable. I mean, the sheer
richness of the material...

Woman talking to Rick:I loved your characterisation of Aileen. There
aren't enough strong women in fiction.

Rick:Actually, I do tend to regard myself as a feminist writer.

Woman:So tell me -- where do you get your ideas?

Page 12 panel 2

BOTTOM TIER -- THREE PANELS. AN EXPENSIVE GENTLEMAN'S CLUB,
DIMLY LIT. TALKING TOGETHER ARE RICK AND A PRODUCER, A TUBBY
TYPE, WITH A HUGE SHOCK OF WHITE HAIR, SMOKING A HUGE CIGAR
(SOME OF THEM DO). THEY'RE SITTING OVER A LITTLE TABLE, WITH A
COUPLE OF DRINKS ON IT.

caption:June 87.

Rick:Harvey, the only condition under which I'd be willing to do a
screenplay for you of "...And My Love," would be if I could direct it.

Harvey:Let me put this simply for you, Ric. Impossible.

Page 12 panel 3

WE'RE OUT ON A LONDON PAVEMENT AT NIGHT, WITH THE LIGHTS
TWINKLING OFF ROMANTICALLY INTO THE DISTANCE. RICK IS
WALKING WITH A BEAUTIFUL YOUNG WOMAN WITH BROWN HAIR --
OBVIOUSLY NOT CALLIOPE -- POSSIBLY WEARING GLASSES.
THEY'RE WEARING LIGHT CLOTHES -- SHE'S IN A SILKY SORT OF
EVENING DRESS. THEY'RE WALKING AWAY FROM US. HE'S
RESTING ONE HAND ON HER BOTTOM, POSSESSIVELY AND JUST A
LITTLE OFFENSIVELY. SHE'S OBVIOUSLY HERO-WORSHIPPING HIM.

Cap:July 1987.

Her:When they said in the TLS that you could be considered the
greatest epic poet since Byron--

Rick:It surprised the hell out of me. I saw The Spirit Who Had Half of
Everything as a lightweight project between real books...

I was honestly surprised when my publisher agreed to take it.

An oblique James Branch Cabell reference. "The Spirit Who Had Half of Everything" was a chapter he never got around to writing in "Figures of Earth".

Page 12 panel 4

WE'RE IN RICK'S STUDY. HE'S TALKING ON A MOBILE PHONE NOW,
NOT THE OLD PHONE HE WAS ON BEFORE, POSSIBLY SITTING IN A
LARGE LEATHER CHAIR. BUT KEEP A COUPLE OF THINGS THE SAME
-- A LITTLE STONE SCULPTURE OF ATHENE, OR SOMETHING. HE'S
GOT A NEW HAIRCUT, NOW, AND LOOKS A LOT SLICKER.

Cap:October 1988.

Rick:Look, Harry, it's nothing that you've done. It's just that the
William Morris agency can look after my interests better. They've got
contacts you haven't.

But you've still got the first three novels and the poetry collection to
handle...

Rick:Don't be like that, Harry.

Page 13 panel 1

OKAY -- STRAIGHT SIX-PANEL GRID, THREE ON TOP, THREE BELOW.
FIRST PANEL -- WE'RE ON A STAGE -- AND UNDER THE SPOTLIGHT
STANDS RICK IN HIS TUXEDO, HOLDING A BIG BOUQUET OF
FLOWERS. HE'S TALKING INTO THE MICROPHONE; WE CAN SEE A
THEATRE SET BEHIND HIM. POSSIBLY DO THIS AS A FAIRLY LONG
SHOT, SO WE CAN SEE THE HEADS OF THE THEATRE-GOING
AUDIENCE.

Cap:February 1989

Rick:Thank you, all of you, so much. You know, when I first told my agent I was planning to write a play, he said Ric, you're crazy.

Rick:So I got a new agent. Ha ha ha.

Page 13 panel 2

SAME CHARACTER AS PAGE 12 PANEL 2: THE PRODUCER, IN AN OFFICE, WITH A DIFFERENT CIGAR. RICK (ALL RIGHT, WE'LL CALL HIM RIC, SINCE THAT'S WHAT HE CALLS HIMSELF), RIC IS WEARING SOMETHING LARGE AND WHITE AND SHARP. HE'S FAR MORE COMFORTABLE THAN HE LOOKED ON THE PREVIOUS PAGE, WHILE THE PRODUCER IS BEING FAR LESS CONDESCENDING.

Caption:April 1989.
Producer:...we've been actively discussing your original offer to write a screenplay, if we let you direct. I'm pleased to tell you that--

Ric:Harvey, it's too late. I've already signed a three-film deal in the US. But thanks, y'know.

Page 13 panel 3

A LARGE HOUSE. SOMEWHERE PRETTY OLD AND IMPRESSIVE. EXTERNAL SHOT. DAYLIGHT. WE CAN SEE AN ATTIC WINDOW AT THE TOP, BARRED, BUT NO-ONE IN THERE.

Caption:May 1989.

Caption:Ric Madoc buys a new house, in Chelsea. He's busy on pre-production for the film, and most of the moving is done for him.

Caption:He moves his most valuable possession himself, though, late one spring night.

Page 13 panel 4

RIC, COOL AND COLLECTED ON A US TV SHOW -- WHATEVER YOUR LOCAL EARLY MORNING TV SHOW IS, CHATTING TO SOMEONE ON A SOFA. WAKE UP AMERICA TYPE LOGO BEHIND THEM. THE ANNOUNCER IS LOOKING AT THE CAMERA, NOT AT RIC.

Cap:September 1989

Ric:No. No, I like Hollywood well enough, but I'm really pleased to be going home. Two months away is enough for me.

Announcer:Hi! In case you've just tuned in, I'm talking to Ric Madoc, writer, poet and soon-to-be film director, about his new epic novel Eagle Stones...

Eagle Stones are stones with magical properties, once said to have been found in eagles' nests. Without the stones the eggs would not hatch.

Page 13 panel 5

NOW WE'RE LOOKING AT A TV SET, AT A SLICK PRESENTER OF U.S. TV SHOW
THE TRAILER, WHICH SHOWS TRAILERS OF UPCOMING MOVIES. HE'S SOME
SLICK IDIOT, WITH 'THE TRAILER' IN THE BACKGROUND. YOU CAN SET THE TV
WHEREVER YOU LIKE, AS LONG AS THE LOCATION'S IN THE US OF A.

Cap:October 1989

Announcer:...Writer of the best-selling novel 'Eagle Stones' talks to us about his
extraordinary new film, "...And the Madness of Crowds," and we'll be showing
some exclusive footage!
That's all... after this short break.

Ric took the title from a Victorian called "Extraordinary Popular Delusions and the Madness of Crowds", by Charles Mackay.

Page 13 panel 6

WE'RE LOOKING AT A MOVIE POSTER -- BASICALLY HAVE FUN DESIGNING IT. I
IMAGINE THAT IT'S A NUMBER OF FACES STARING BLANKLY OUT AT US.
LARGE ON IT IS THE TITLE RIC MADOC'S '...AND THE MADNESS OF CROWDS,'
AND THERE'S A FLASH ACROSS THE BOTTOM RIGHT HAND CORNER, READING
NOMINATED FOR 3 OSCARS. BEST ORIGINAL SCREENPLAY, BEST DIRECTOR, AND
BEST PICTURE.

TODD -- YOU'LL PROBABLY WANT TO DO THE LETTERING FOR THIS. DO IT LIKE
A FAIRLY CLASSY MOVIE POSTER. THINK WOODY ALLEN, I SUPPOSE.

Caption:March 1990.

ON A FENCE — NOT BRICK.

Page 14 panel 1

I'LL STICK TO THE SAME KIND OF GRID STRUCTURE HERE, BUT FEEL FREE TO
LOOSEN IT UP NOW, SINCE WE'RE IN REAL TIME. WE'RE NOW IN THE ATTIC OF
THE NEW HOUSE. WE'RE LOOKING AT CALLIOPE. SHE'S NOW SORT OF DRESSED -
- A LIGHT BLOUSE, AND A SKIRT, ALTHOUGH SHE'S BAREFOOT. THE WALLS ARE
BARE, AND, BEHIND HER, WE CAN SEE THE WINDOW, BARRED. IT'S NOT AS
TACKY AS THE ROOM WE SAW BEFORE, IN WHICH SHE WAS IMPRISONED, BUT
NEITHER IS IT FURNISHED IN ANY WAY. SHE'S LOOKING STRAIGHT TOWARD US.
SHE LOOKS A LITTLE SURPRISED. A LITTLE STARTLED. ALSO A LITTLE
NERVOUS. THIS IS FROM THE SANDMAN'S VIEWPOINT, SO WE CAN'T ACTUALLY
SEE THE SANDMAN.

Calliope:Oh. It's you.

Page 14 panel 2

I always refer to him in scripts as The Sandman, though that's not his name...

SANDMAN'S VIEWPOINT AGAIN. SHE'S LOOKING DOWN, NOW, A LITTLE
EMBARRASSED PERHAPS. IT'S BEEN FOUR THOUSAND YEARS SINCE SHE'S HAD
ANYTHING TO DO WITH HIM, AND THEY DIDN'T PART ON THE BEST OF TERMS.

Calliope:They... they told me that you had been imprisoned. Just like me.

Sandman caption:They spoke the truth. I was imprisoned. But, as you can see, I am free now.

Page 14 panel 3

RIGHT -- SAME VIEWPOINT, BUT SHE'S TAKEN A STEP TOWARD US, NERVOUSLY, BUT URGENTLY.

calliope:Then please -- by the love I once had for you. By -- whatever you felt for me. Please.

Make him give me my freedom. Make him let me go.
Page 14 panel 4

WE'RE IN A TV STUDIO, AND THE LOGO BEHIND US READS "THE BOOK NOOK." AN INTERVIEWER SITS IN A CHAIR, WEARING A HAT, WITH A HANDLEBAR MOUSTACHE. ON THE TABLE BETWEEN THEM ARE GLASSES OF WATER, AND PERHAPS A COUPLE OF BOOKS. HE'S EXPOUNDING. RIC SITS ON A CHAIR NEXT TO HIM. WE MAY BE ABLE TO SEE A FEW CAMERAMEN WITH CAMERAS AROUND.

The interviewer bears an resemblance

Interviewer:Although you've been compared to the multi-talented Jean Cocteau, and to a lesser extent to writer-directors like Clive Barker, it seems to me that the creator who perhaps you most resemble is the late 1940's cult figure, Erasmus Fry...

friend and sometime collaborator, Kim Newman.

Page 14 panel 5

CLOSE IN ON RIC. HE LOOKS A LITTLE PERTURBED. HE'S LEANING FORWARD, ONE FINGER RAISED. BY NOW RIC HAS A TOTALLY NEW IMAGE THAT HE'S COMFORTABLE WITH -- ONE EARRING PERHAPS, HIS RED HAIR CUT VERY SHORT AT THE SIDES, LONGER AT THE BACK.

Big Shot. Lotsa Shadow

Ric:Excuse me -- you said 'the late.' He's dead?

Interviewer:Last summer. Did you know him?

From here ON - ALL shots of Rick close or cropped, more ANXIETY in Atmosphere

Page 14 panel 6

PULL BACK AGAIN INTO A TWO SHOT. RIC'S SITTING BACK IN HIS CHAIR, A LITTLE STUNNED.

Ric:I didn't know him. We met... on a couple of occasions. He was... interested in my work.

Interviewer:Ah. Anyway, like you, Fry was above all a creator of epics, of huge, towering romances...

Page 15 panel 1

AFTER THE TAPING'S OVER, THE INTERVIEWER IS TALKING WITH RIC IN THE
BBC BAR, AND SINCE I'M NOT GOING TO GET YOU PHOTOREF OF THE BBC BAR,
JUST IMAGINE ANY SMALL BAR, VERY HIGH CLASS WITHOUT BEING POSH, AND
YOU'LL DO FINE. THEY'RE STANDING TOGETHER, BOTH WITH DRINKS IN THEIR
HANDS.

Interviewer:...went very well, I thought. It'll be broadcast in June -- we'll let you
know the exact date.

Ric:Thanks.

I suppose Fry must have died when I was shooting in the US. Old age, I suppose.
He must've been almost ninety.

Page 15 panel 2

CLOSE IN ON THE INTERVIEWER. HE'S JUST TALKING CASUALLY -- AS FAR AS
HE'S CONCERNED THIS IS JUST A GOOD ANECDOTE.

Interviewer:Oh no. He poisoned himself.

It's quite funny. Apparently the last thing he did was write a letter to his old
publishers, begging them to bring one of his books back into print...

Page 15 panel 3

PULL BACK AGAIN FOR A TWO SHOT, OR CLOSE IN ON RIC. HE LOOKS A LITTLE
GUILTY, A LITTLE HURT.

Ric:'Here Comes A Candle,' I suppose.

Interviewer:I think that was it. How did you guess?

Ric:It was a good book. Perhaps my favourite book, when
 I was growing up.

Very moving, and honest, and strange.

Ric:Poor old sod.

Page 15 panel 4

OUTSIDE THE HOUSE WE SAW ON PAGE 13 PANEL 3. A CAR IS PARKED
IN FRONT OF THE HOUSE, AND RIC IS GETTING OUT AND SHUTTING
THE DOOR.

No dialogue.

Handwritten notes:

Again Lotsa shadow — almost silhouette.

After this story was published, my friend Pete Atkins told me that "Here Comes A Candle" was the title of his first-published story. I had to confess I hadn't known that before. But Pete's mind and mine often run* in similar directions...

* or hop. Or shuffle.

Page 15 panel 5

RIC, OPENING THE FRONT DOOR, WITH HIS FRONT DOOR KEY. UP TO YOU
REALLY HOW YOU DO THIS PANEL, AND THE TWO ON EITHER SIDE -- BASICALLY
WE'RE JUST SPENDING THREE SILENT PANELS WATCHING HIM GO INTO HIS
HOUSE. WE'RE ALSO BUILDING UP THE SUSPENSE A BIT, BECAUSE DEEP IN
THEIR GUTS, THE READER KNOWS THAT WHEN WE TURN THE PAGE, THE
SANDMAN'S GOING TO BE THERE, AND INDEED HE IS. SO MAKE THESE THREE
PANELS AS PROSAIC AS POSSIBLE. IT'S LIKE THE MOMENT IN A MOVIE WHEN
YOU SUDDENLY NOTICE THAT THE MUSICAL SOUNDTRACK HAS STOPPED, AND
ALL WE CAN HEAR ARE HIS FEET CRUNCHING ON THE GRAVEL, THE KEYS IN
THE LOCK, HIS FOOTSTEPS ECHOING MUFFLED DOWN THE HALL.

No dialogue.

Page 15 panel 6

RIC, PROBABLY FROM BEHIND, WALKING DOWN A CORRIDOR.
No dialogue.

Page 16. Panel 1

OKAY. OVER THE PAGE. WE'RE LOOKING AT THE SANDMAN. NOW, LOOKING AT
SANDMAN 13, WITH ALL THE VARIANT CLOTHES THROUGH THE YEARS,
SHOWED ME THAT THE CHARACTER LOOKS PRETTY GOOD HOWEVER HE'S
DRESSED, AND I'VE WANTED TO EXPERIMENT A LITTLE, FOR A WHILE. SO, HOW
HE'S DRESSED: HE'S DRESSED IN BLACK. YOU'LL PROBABLY WANT TO
ACTUALLY BLACK IN AS MUCH AS POSSIBLE OF THIS, AND NOTE ON THE
ARTWORK THAT THE REST OF IT'S IN K-TONE GREYS, OTHERWISE ROBBIE WILL
PROBABLY DO HIM IN PURPLE, WHICH THE SEPARATORS WILL PRINT PINK FOR
NO IMMEDIATELY OBVIOUS REASON... ANYWAY, THIS IS WHAT HE LOOKS LIKE.
FACIALLY, AND HAIR-WISE, NOTHING MUCH HAS CHANGED -- STILL A SHOCK
MOP OF BLACK HAIR, AND A LONG, THIN, SLIGHTLY ANDROGYNOUS FACE WITH
GOOD CHEEKBONES AND NO EYES -- JUST BLACK SHADOWS WHERE THE EYES
SHOULD BE WITH, OCCASIONALLY, LONE AND DISTANT SINGLE STARS GLINTING
IN THE SOCKETS. BUT INSTEAD OF WEARING A BLACK COAT, PUT HIM IN A
LARGE BLACK LEATHER JACKET, WITH A HIGH COLLAR IN THE BACK, THIN
BLACK JEANS, AND A JET-BLACK TEE SHIRT. HE DOMINATES ANY ROOM HE'S
IN: HE'S REGAL, ARISTOCRATIC; ALTHOUGH IN A LEATHER JACKET HE LOOKS
MORE LIKE THE SKINNY, UNDEAD KING OF THE STYLE BIKER PUNKS FROM
HELL. HE'S SITTING ON A CHAIR, WITH HIS ARMS CROSSED, AND LEGS
CROSSED, LOOKING FAIRLY COMFORTABLE. HAVING SAID THAT, HE IS NOT
PLEASED -- THE IMPRISONMENT ASPECT REMINDS HIM TOO MUCH OF HIS OWN
IMPRISONMENT. IMAGINE A PARENT, OR A COP, WAITING FOR YOU TO COME
HOME. IF HE'S NEXT TO A TABLE ONE OF HIS ARMS COULD BE ON THE TABLE,
PERHAPS. HE'S LOOKING UP AT RIC, EITHER ON THE EXTREME LEFT OR OFF
PANEL TO THE LEFT. OH -- THE LOUNGE -- GO FOR THAT LARGE, SPACIOUS,
UNLIVED-IN SORT OF LOOK YOU GET IN MAGAZINES, BUT ONLY EVER REALLY
GET BY NOT LIVING SOMEWHERE. POSSIBLY A FEW HUGE PAINTINGS ON THE
WALL, DEPICTING CLASSICAL SCENES -- PERSEUS CUTTING OFF THE GORGON'S
HEAD, FOR EXAMPLE. *SANDMAN IS NIGHT'S FACE*

Ric (off, left):Christ! What are you doing in my house?

Who let you in?

Sandman:Nobody let me in, Richard Madoc.

Page 16 panel 2

WE'RE LOOKING AT RICK, IN MEDIUM CLOSE UP -- HE'S ANGRY, IS GESTURING TOWARDS US, WHITE WITH ANGER AND THE SHOCK YOU GET WHEN YOU FIND A STRANGER IN YOUR HOME. TIGHT-LIPPED.

Like me knows the deal and is Guilt Ridden

Ric:I don't know who you are, but I want you out of here, now, or I'm calling the police.

Page 16 panel 3

BOTTOM TIER. LONG, THIN PANEL; AN EXTREME CLOSE-UP ON THE SANDMAN'S FACE. DARK SHADOWY EYES, WITH SINGLE STAR GLINTING IN ONE EYE. HE'S REASONABLY ANGRY AS WELL, BUT THE SANDMAN GETS QUIETLY ANGRY, NOT LOUDLY ANGRY.

Sandman:Be quiet.

Page 16 panel 4

OKAY -- THE SANDMAN HAS STOOD UP, NOW. WE'VE GOT A TWO SHOT -- THE SANDMAN'S STOOD UP, NOW. HE'S ON LEFT OF PANEL, HIS BACK SLIGHTLY TO US, FACING THE SANDMAN, IS ON THE RIGHT. THE SANDMAN IS ABOUT 6'4" AT THIS POINT, RIC IS ABOUT 5'11", SO THAT RIC IS LOOKING UP AT THE SANDMAN. IF THE SANDMAN'S ARMS WEREN'T FOLDED BEFORE, THEY ARE NOW.

Sandman:You are keeping a woman imprisoned here, Richard Madoc. Keeping her against her will.

I have come to request that you set her free.

Page 17 panel 1

FOUR PANELS ON THE TOP TIER. SMALL PANEL -- RIC, TRYING TO BLUSTER IT OUT. HEAD SHOT.

Ric:Are you out of your mind? There's no woman here. Now get out of here. Do you know who I am? There -- there's a law against people like you.

Page 17 panel 2

SAME SIZED PANEL. THE SANDMAN, HEAD AND SHOULDERS, STARING AT US. HE'S NOT SAYING ANYTHING. HIS EXPRESSION IS BLANK. HE KNOWS MADOC IS

LYING.

No dialogue.

Page 17 panel 3

SAME SHOT AS PANEL 1. RIC, LOOKING DOWN; HE'S REALLY WORRIED. HE'S
REALLY FRIGHTENED. HE KNOWS HE CAN'T BLUFF THIS ONE OUT.

Ric:Are you going to call the police? Is that it?

Page 17 panel 4
THE SANDMAN -- LOOKING STRAIGHT AT US, HEAD SHOT AGAIN. HE'S JUST
STATING THE FACTS.

SM:No. I will not call any human agency.

SM:Just let her go.

page 17 panel 5

PANEL ALONG THE MIDDLE OF THE PAGE. LONG PANEL -- ON THE LEFT IS RIC,
LOOKING DOWN, LOOKING SHAKEN, AND BROKEN. HE'S ABOUT TEN FEET AWAY
FROM US. ON THE EXTREME RIGHT, FAIRLY CLOSE TO US, WE CAN SEE THE
SANDMAN'S FACE IN PROFILE.

Ric:But you don't understand -- I need her. If I didn't have her, I wouldn't be able
to write. I wouldn't have ideas.

I can't free her yet. Not now. Maybe in a year or so.

Look, I have money -- an awful lot of money -- and ...

SM:Hold your tongue.

Page 17 panel 6

TWO PANELS ON THE BOTTOM TIER. HEAD SHOT OF THE SANDMAN, STARING
STRAIGHT AT US: HE SEEMS HALF AMUSED, HALF DISGUSTED, HALF HURT.
(YES, I KNOW IT MAKES THREE HALVES.) IT's okay -I FAILed math ⨧

SM:She has been held captive for more than sixty years. Stripped of all
posessions. Demeaned, abused, and hurt.

I... know how she must feel.

SM:And you will not free her, because 'you need the ideas'?

Page 17 panel 7
OK -- NOW GO IN FOR THE FINAL PANEL FOR A REALLY CLOSE-CLOSE UP: ONE
EYE, STARING AT US, WITH A LITTLE WHITE SKIN AROUND IT.

SM:You disgust me, Richard Madoc.

SM:You want ideas? You want dreams? You want stories?
Then ideas you will have.

Ideas in abundance.

Page 18 panel 1

WE'RE OPPOSITE AN AD PAGE HERE, AND THE FIRST PANEL'S A SMALLISH
PANEL, SHOWING RIC. HE'S RAISED HIS HAND TO HIS FACE. HE'S WAKING UP --
HE WAS ASLEEP. SITTING IN A LARGE ARMCHAIR, IF WE CAN SEE IT. THIS IS A
CLOSE-UP ON HIS FACE. THIS PAGE IS ROUGHLY A NINE-PANEL GRID.

Ric:Uhhhnn.

Page 18 panel 2

LARGER PANEL. IT WOULD COVER TWO PANELS OF A NINE PANEL GRID. THE
ROOM -- THE SAME ROOM WE WERE IN ON THE PAGE BEFORE. RIC'S GETTING
UP FROM HIS CHAIR, WIPING HIS EYES. THE SIZE OF THE ROOM, THE
CLEANLINESS AND CLEAN LINES, EMPHASISE THE EMPTINESS OF THE ROOM,
AND THE FACT THE ONLY PERSON IN IT IS RIC HIMSELF. HE'S POSSIBLY
RUBBING HIS EYES, POSSIBLY LOOKIING AROUND THE ROOM. VERY CLEAN
LINES -- ALMOST MOEBIUS-LIKE.

No dialogue.

Page 18 panel 3

NEXT TIER. OKAY -- NOW WE'RE UPSTAIRS IN THE ROOM WHERE SHE'S BEING
KEPT PRISONER. WE'RE LOOKING STRAIGHT AT RIC. NOW FOR THE FIRST TIME
IN A WHILE WE CAST SHADOWS UP HIS FACE, PROBABLY LIGHTING HIM FROM
BELOW. REAL BRIDE OF FRANKENSTEIN STUFF. HE LOOKS A LITTLE HAUNTED.

Ric:I just had this weird dream....

What do you know about it? Huh? Are you doing that? Giving me nightmares?

Are you doing it?

Page 18 panel 4

WE'RE LOOKING AT CALLIOPE, WHO'S JUST STARING UP AT US SULLENLY.

No dialogue.

Page 18 panel 5

POSSIBLY DO THIS FROM CALLIOPE'S VIEWPOINT. RIC HAS RAISED HIS FIST. HE
LOOKS A LITTLE CRAZY. HIS EYES ARE WIDE, HIS NOSTRILS FLARED. HE'S

REALLY READY TO BEAT THE SHIT OUT OF HER.

Ric:Tell me.

Ric:Tell me, or so help me, I'll, I'll...

Page 18 panel 6

CALLIOPE, IN CLOSE UP, TALKING, LOOKING TOWARD US, OR
SLIGHTLY TO THE LEFT. SHE LOOKS PROUD, LIKE SHE'S PULLED
WHATEVER REMNANTS OF DIGNITY SHE HAS AROUND HER,
BECAUSE SHE KNOWS THAT RIC'S TIME HAS COME.

Calliope:No, I am not doing it, Richard Madoc.

A possible etymology of "Morpheus" is "He who shapes"...

You have met Oneiros, whom the Romans called the Shaper of Form.

Calliope:He was once my lover, and he was the father of my son.
Ric (off, small):I didn't know you'd ever had a son.

Page 18 panel 7

PULL BACK -- REALLY LONG SHOT. OF THE TWO OF THEM. TWO
TINY FIGURES -- HE'S NEARER TO US, SHE'S TURNED TO THE
WINDOW.

SHe should BE Looking out of tHE wiNdow Like she's waiting foR something

Calliope:You know nothing about me, Richard Madoc.

I am alive in my own right. I am more than a receptacle for
your seed, or an inspiration for your tales.

Page 18 panel 8

A line I changed on the second draft of the script, but that been left as it was originally in the lettered version.

ANOTHER LONG SHOT. HE'S WALKING TOWARD US, SEEMING
PUZZLED AND WEIRDED OUT. SHE'S IN THE BACKGROUND, STARING
OUT OF THE WINDOW, SADLY. SHE'S NOT LOOKING AT HIM.

Calliope:Still, it is too late now to let that concern you.

Calliope:Goodbye, Richard Madoc. Enjoy your party.

Page 19, panel 1

OKAY -- OVER THE PAGE, NOW: I TEND TO IMAGINE THE NEXT TWO
PAGES AS BEING LAID OUT BY EARLY SWAMP THING BISSETTE AND
TOTLEBEN, ALL PANEL ANGLES JAGGED AND ANGULAR, AS IF THE
PAGE IS A HUGE SHATTERED MIRROR. DON'T DO PANELS 19 AND
20 AS A DOUBLE PAGE SPREAD, COS WHEN OR IF IT'S EVER
COLLECTED UP, 19 IS OPPOSITE 18, WHICH ISN'T TRUE HERE.
WE'RE LOOKING AT A SMALLISH PANEL. RICK IS CLOSE TO US, AND
IN FRONT OF HIM, FURTHER AWAY FROM US, IS A NEWSPAPER-

SELLER, ON A PAPER STALL. RIC'S DRESSED AS HE WAS BEFORE -- IT'S NOW
LATE AFTERNOON, EARLY AFTERNOON. HE'S TAKING A MAGAZINE AND A
NEWSPAPER.

Ric:A Time Out, please. And a Standard.

Paperman:Right-ho. Saw you on the telly the other night. I said to my wife, he
buys papers from me, she said, He never, I said, he does. One twenty, please.

RIc: Ah... I'm going to a party...

Page 19 panel 2

OKAY -- BEGIN TO DISTORT THINGS. RIC'S LOOKING TOWARDS US, INTENTLY,
POSSIBLY IN REAL CLOSE-UP. HE'S CRACKING UP -- IS EXCITED AND OBSESSED.

Ric:You know, I could write a whole story set at a party. Possibly something could
have happened to the world outside -- a holocaust of some kind...
These people are partying against the darkness.

Page 19 panel 3

RIC IS STUMBLING TOWARDS US DOWN THE PAVEMENT, TOWARDS OUR TILTED
CAMERA, ACROSS A JAGGED PANEL BORDER -- POSSIBLY WE CAN SEE THE
NEWSPAPERSELLER IN THE BACKGROUND, WAVING, WORRIEDLY.

Newspaperman (smallish):Here! Mister Madoc! That's one pound twenty you owe
me!

Ric:The fraternity of critics. In reality a dark brethren, linked by profane rites and
blood vows. To destroy an author they sacrifice a child and perform a critical
mass...

Page 19 panel 4

OKAY -- RIC'S NOW GRABBED SOMEONE, POSSIBLY A LITTLE OLD LADY, BY THE
LAPELS, AND, OBSESSED AND CRAZED, IS PULLING HER UP OFF THE GROUND,
SHOUTING IN HER FACE. SHE'S TERRIFIED, NOT SAYING ANYTHING.

Ric:A city in which the streets are paved with time.

Ric:A train full of silent women, plunging forever through the twilight.

Ric:Heads made of light. A small piece of blue cardboard. A plum,
sweet and tart and cold. A were-goldfish who transforms into a wolf
at full moon.

I may write this story one day.

Page 19 panel 5

LONG PANEL. HALF AN HOUR LATER. OKAY -- A CROWDED SIDEWALK, AND
RIC'S CRAWLING ON THE GROUND TOWARD US. PEOPLE AROUND ARE STANDING
AND LOOKING AT HIM -- NO-ONE'S DOING ANYTHING TO HELP HIM. HIS CLOTHES

ARE LOOKING FRAYED AND DIRTY AS IF HE'S BEEN CLIMBING AROUND ON THE
SIDEWALK FOR HALF AN HOUR. HIS FINGERNAILS HAVE BEEN WORN DOWN
AND THE TIPS OF HIS FINGERS ARE BLEEDING. EITHER IN THIS PANEL OR ONE
OF THE NEXT FEW, YOU COULD SHOW A WALL WITH, OVER IT, ON A RED
OVERLAY, SOME KIND OF WEIRD IMPRESSIONISTIC DRAWING, LOOKING LIKE IT
WAS EXECUTED WITH RED PAINT.

TODD-- THE LETTERING'S GRADUALLY GETTING WAVIER, AS RIC LOSES HIS
GRIP ON EVERYTHING. WAVERY ALL THROUGH.

Ric:Two old women taking a weasel on holiday.

Ric: Gryphons shouldn't marry. Vampires don't dance.

Ric:A man who inherits a library card to the library at Alexandria.

Ric:A rose bush, a nightingale, and a black rubber dog- collar.

Page 20 panel 1

OKAY, STILL REALLY JAGGEDY PANELS. AND WE CAN SEE THE PREVIOUS
SCENE FROM A BIT OF A DISTANCE NOW. A MAN -- FELIX GARRISON -- FOUR
YEARS OLDER, IS WALKING WITH HIS BACK TO US, ATTRACTED BY A KNOT OF
PEOPLE STANDING AROUND THE FALLEN MAN.

Ric: (small and wavery):A man who falls in love with a paper doll.

The sun setting over the Parthenon. Shark's teeth soup.

*People should do nothing
but watch — look
EERIE R*

Felix:Is something wrong? I'm a doctor. Stand back, please.

Page 20 panel 2

FELIX LEANING OVER RIC, WHO'S NOW LYING ON HIS BACK ON THE SIDEWALK,
STILL TOTALLY HYPER AND OBSESSED. FELIX, WHO WE CAN NOW RECOGNISE,
IS SHOCKED, BUT, BEING A GOOD DOCTOR, SIMPLY LOOKS CONCERNED, NOT
UPSET.

Felix:Good grief -- Richard Madoc!

What's the matter, old fellow?

Ric: (wavery)I'm just having ideas. So many...

Ric:(wavery)An old man in Sunderland who owned the universe, and who kept it
in a jam-jar in the dusty cupboard under his stairs...

Page 20 panel 3

OKAY -- RIC IS NOW SORT OF STANDING UP, LEANING HEAVILY ON FELIX,

WHO'S THROWN RIC'S ARM OVER HIS SHOULDER. HE'S STAGGERING DOWN THE
PAVEMENT, SUPPORTING MUCH OF RIC'S WEIGHT, WHILE AROUND THEM (IF
YOU CAN GET THEM IN) SPECTATORS JUST STAND AND STARE, MAKING NO
EFFORT TO DO ANYTHING AT ALL. IF YOU CAN'T GET THE SPECTATORS IN THEN
DON'T WORRY AND DON'T PUSH IT.

Felix:My home is just around the corner. Lean on me. Do you remember me --
Felix Garrison?

Ric:(wavery)It's the ideas. Where we get them from. A sestina about silence, using
the key words Dark, Ragged, Never, Screaming, Fire, Kiss *strangely enough,*
people actually did
write sestinas using

Page 20 panel 4

FELIX IS PUSHING OPEN HIS FRONT DOOR, WITH RIC JUST SORT OF CLUTCHING
HIM. RIC HAS ONE ARM OVER FELIX'S SHOULDER -- FELIX IS TAKING ALL HIS
WEIGHT. RIC OBVIOUSLY JUST DOESN'T HAVE MUCH FREE ATTENTION, HE'S
STARING OFF IN SOME OTHER DIMENSION, TALKING TO HIMSELF, TALKING.
FELIX GARRISON F.R.C.S. ON A BRONZE PLATE ON THE DOOR.

I think if I'd

Felix:Come on inside. You'll have to tell me what's the matter. Soon have you
feeling better... *known anyone was*

actually going to
Ric: (wavery) A biography of Keats, from the Lamia's viewpoint...

attempt it, I'd've
Page 20 panel 5
made it a triolet or

OKAY -- INSIDE FELIX'S HOUSE. RIC IS NOW SITTING IN A LARGE LEATHER
CHAIR, STARING HOPELESSLY IN FRONT OF HIM -- HE'S NOT FOCUSING ON
ANYTHING, STARING OFF BLANKLY. HE'S RAISED HIS HANDS TO HIS FACE, AND
WE CAN SEE THAT THE ENDS OF THE FINGERS ARE REALLY DISGUSTING -- HE'S
ALMOST WORN THEM DOWN -- THEY'RE ALMOST JUST NUBS OF BLOODY MEAT,
CRACKED FINGERNAILS. FELIX HAS REACHED DOWN AND IS TOUCHING ONE OF
THE HANDS, ALTHOUGH I SUSPECT HE'S STANDING UP, AND GOES OFF ABOVE
THE TOP OF THE PANEL, SO IT'S PROBABLY JUST HIS ONE ARM, COMING FROM
OFF PANEL. TODD -- NOT WAVERY ANY MORE.

Felix:God -- what did you do to your hands?

Ric:All the pictures in my head. I had to get them down, but I didn't have any
paper, or paints. So I used a wall.

And my fingertips.

Page 21 panel 1

ANOTHER STANDALONE PAGE OPPOSITE AN ADVERT. OKAY -- NOW REGULARISE
THE PANELS. WE'RE IN FELIX'S HOUSE. LONG SHOT OF THE TWO MEN -- RIC IS
SITTING DOWN, FELIX IS STANDING UP, GETTING A BOTTLE OF PILLS OUT OF A
CABINET OR SOMETHING.

Ric: All the ideas, inside. All the pictures and poems and tales and songs and plays and speeches and fragments...

They're all coming out. You must help me.

Felix: I'll give you a sedative. And I'll bandage those fingers.

Ric: No! No... I'm sorry. Nothing like that.

Page 21 panel 2

GO IN FOR AN EXTREME CLOSE-UP OF RIC'S FACE, TORTURED AND UNHAPPY.

Ric: It's her revenge, you see. Or his revenge. I said I needed the ideas -- but they're coming so fast, swamping me, overwhelming me...

You have to make them stop.

Page 21 panel 3

WE CAN SEE FELIX'S OUTSTRETCHED HAND, WITH THREE PILLS IN THE PALM.

Felix: Here -- this will calm your nerves.

Concentrate on Ric's hands

Ric: No! I told you.

Look -- go to my house. The keys are in my pocket if - if you can take them out for me. I don't think I can use my hands any more.

Page 21 panel 4

RIC IN MEDIUM CLOSE-UP, OR A TWO-SHOT OF THE BOTH OF THEM. HE'S PLEADING WITH FELIX. FELIX COULD BE HOLDING THE DOOR KEYS.

Ric: Go upstairs. At the top of the house there's a room. There's a woman in there.

Let her out. She's locked up in there, you see.

Page 21 panel 5

FELIX IS PUTTING ON HIS COAT. NEARER TO US, RIC SITS IN THE CHAIR, IN HIS OWN LITTLE UNIVERSE, STARING AT US AS WELL. HIS EYES ARE LARGE AND WHITE AND ROUND, HIS PUPILS ALMOST PINPRICKS; HE'S HALF TALKING TO HIMSELF, HALF TO FELIX. FELIX IS READY TO GO. HE LOOKS CONCERNED.

Ric: Tell her -- tell her that she can go. That I free her. Make her leave. Make her go away.

Ric: I signed a book for you once, didn't I?

Oh god. Please.

Page 21 panel 6

FELIX IS OVER BY THE DOOR, IN THE BACKGROUND, FACING US. RIC IS STILL IN
THE CHAIR, STARING OFF INTO THE UNFOCUSED DISTANCE. FACE SCRATCHED,
CLOTHES TORN, HANDS RUINED.

Felix:All right. Stay there. I'll be back soon.

Ric:Make it stop. Tell her I'm sorry.

Ric:Magical and alchemical traditions seen as a cargo cult; Aureolus Theophrastus
Bombastes Paracelsus and Raymond Lulli were the same man.

page 22 panel 1

OK -- OUTSIDE SHOT OF RIC'S HOUSE. IT'S NOW EVENING -- ABOUT THREE OR
FOUR HOURS LATER THAN OUR LAST GLIMPSE OF THE HOUSE. NOT A BIG
PANEL. WE CAN SEE FELIX GOING IN.

No dialogue.

Page 22 panel 2

OK -- NOW DO AN ANGLE SHOT, SO WE CAN SEE UPWARDS, UP A SPIRAL
STAIRCASE, AND, AT THE TOP OF THE STAIRS, IS FELIX, OPENING A DOOR --
THE ROOM WHERE CALLIOPE HAS BEEN KEPT PRISONER. HE'S UNDOING A
PADLOCK.

Felix:Um. Hello?

Felix:Is there, um, anyone here? He says -- Ric, uh, says you're free to go. Hello?

Page 22 panel 3

OKAY -- NOW, WE'RE IN A ROOM, WHICH IS HER CELL. IT'S EMPTY: THERE ARE
BARE WALLS, BARE FLOORBOARDS, A BARRED WINDOW, AND, ON THE FLOOR,
A LARGE, OLD LEATHERBOUND BOOK, WITH A PAPERJACKET. BY OLD, I MEAN
PROBABLY ABOUT FIFTY YEARS OLD. WE CAN EITHER SEE FELIX IN THE ROOM,
OR WE CAN SEE HIS SHADOW COMING IN FROM OUTSIDE. WE SHOULD FEEL
WE'RE ABLE TO SEE ALL THE ROOM, POSSIBLY SLIGHTLY FISH-EYE, AND WE
CAN TELL IT'S EMPTY.

No dialogue.

Page 22 panel 4

WE'RE LOOKING, FROM FELIX'S VIEWPOINT, AT THE BOOK ON THE FLOOR.
IT'S CALLED HERE COMES A CANDLE BY ERASMUS FRY, AND IT'S GOT AN
ILLUSTRATION ON THE FRAYED PAPER JACKET -- AN OLD-FASHIONED,

SLIGHTLY STYLISED ILLUSTRATION SHOWING A YOUNG WOMAN, NAKED BUT ALWAYS DISCREETLY COVERED BY HAIR. THERE'S A BLURB ON THE BOOK-COVER AS WELL, WHICH READS SHE WAS HIS MUSE -- AND THE SLAVE OF HIS LUST!

No dialogue.

Page 22 panel 5

WE CAN SEE FELIX NOW, IN THE ROOM. HE'S PICKED UP THE BOOK, AND HE'S RAISED HIS HAND TO HIS FOREHEAD, LOWERED HIS HEAD; IT'S OBVIOUS TO HIM THAT RIC'S CRACKED UP COMPLETELY BY NOW.

No dialogue.

Page 22 panel 6

WE CAN SEE HIM WALKING AWAY, LOOKING DEJECTED -- HE'S ON HIS WAY TOWARD THE FRONT DOOR. WE'RE LOOKING FROM A SECOND FLOOR STAIRCASE DOWN AT HIM BELOW US. HE'S STILL GOT THE BOOK.

No dialogue.

Page 23 panel 1

OKAY -- NOW, GO FROM A LOT OF SHADING TO VERY STARK WHITES AND BLACKS. NO MORE WEIRD ANGLE SHOTS ON THIS PAGE, EITHER. VERY REGULAR PANEL GRID -- THREE ON THE TOP, THREE ON THE BOTTOM. WE'RE LOOKING AT, ON THE LEFT, CALLIOPE, AND ON THE RIGHT, THE SANDMAN. THEY'RE BOTH LEANING ON THE BANISTER, LOOKING DOWNWARDS, INTERESTED. SHE'S NOW WEARING A LIGHT TUNIC -- A CHITON, I SEEM TO REMEMBER IT'S CALLED, UNLESS THAT'S SOMETHING ELSE, BUT A STANDARD CLASSICAL GREEK TUNIC-SKIRT, AND HER HAIR IS PILED UP ON HER HEAD, BEHIND HER. SHE LOOKS A LOT MORE IN CONTROL. CLEAN AND PERFECT. HE'S WEARING HIS BLACK ROBE, COVERING ALL OF HIM, FROM HEAD TO TOE.

Calliope:So. It's over. Thank you.

SANDMANS CAPE IS ALIVE, FOLDS ARE LIKE INTESTINES.

Sandman:What will you do now, Calliope?

Calliope:I don't know. Return to the minds of humanity,
 I suspect. My time is over, and this age of the world is not my age.

Page 23 panel 2

SHE'S NOW LOOKING UP AT HIM, WHILE HE'S STILL STARING STRAIGHT AHEAD OF HIMSELF. SHE'S LOOKING AT HIM WITH WONDER, OR WITH DEEP THOUGHT.

Calliope:You have changed, Oneiros. In the old days, you would have left me to rot forever, without turning a hair...

Calliope:Do you still hate me? For what I did?

Page 23 panel 3

CLOSE UPON THE SANDMAN -- HE'S NOT LOOKING AT HER, BUT HE'S THINKING,
AND BEING HONEST. AND HE SAYS,

Sandman:No. I no longer hate you, Calliope.

I have learned much in recent times, and...

Sandman:No matter. I do not hate you, child.

Calliope:I think you should release the mortal now. He has set me free...

Sandman:If that is what you wish, it is done.

Page 23 panel 4

PULL BACK AGAIN FOR A TWO SHOT. THEY'RE WALKING DOWN THE STAIRS
TOGETHER, TOWARD THE FRONT HALL, AND WE'RE LOOKING STRAIGHT AT
THEM, AND SHE'S BEGINNING TO SMILE, AND SAYING.

Calliope:Maybe...

Calliope:Maybe I could visit you, in the dream realm? It would be nice to see you
again. Properly. What do you think?

Page 23 panel 5

OKAY -- THEY'RE OUTSIDE THE HOUSE, NOW. AND SHE'S TURNED HER BACK ON
HIM, SO SHE'S FACING RIGHT, AND HE'S LEFT OF HER, FACING RIGHT AS WELL,
LOOKING DOWN AT HER. POSSIBLY REACHING OUT AS IF HE'S ABOUT TO TOUCH
HER, BUT HAS THOUGHT BETTER OF IT.

SM:I do not think that would be a good idea, Calliope.

Calliope:No. No, perhaps it wouldn't.
Thank you anyway, Oneiros. I will not forget this.

Page 23 panel 6

SHE'S NOW FACING US. HE'S SIMPLY FADING AWAY -- HE LOOKS LIKE A
RAGGED SMUDGE OF BLACK -- CHECK SANDMAN 8 PAGE 11 FOR WHAT I'M
TALKING ABOUT HERE (I ASSUME MIKE DID IT BY MOVING A PHOTOCOPY
AROUND) OR THE LAST PAGE OF SANDMAN 3. SHE LOOKS HURT, PERHAPS, AND
THOUGHTFUL.

Calliope: Fare you well, Oneiros. Fortune go with you.
Sandman:Goodbye, Calliope.

Don't like the smudge, looks like mistake - cross hatch

page 24 panel 1

OKAY -- WE'RE BACK IN THE STUDY WE WERE IN BEFORE, FELIX'S PLACE.
SITTING, EYES BLANK AND HUGE, STARING AT US, IS RIC. FELIX IS STANDING
BEHIND HIM. HE NOW HAS NO IDEAS -- THAT'S ALL BEEN TAKEN AWAY FROM
HIM.
Felix:I've done it, Rick. Um, how are you feeling now?

Ric:I... I don't know any more.

I keep trying to think... about what she said...

Ric:`The shaper of forms'... it seems like it should mean something...

Page 24 panel 2

WHITE PANEL. WE CAN SEE, IN THE MEDIUM DISTANCE, THE SANDMAN, IN HIS
CLOAK, BASICALLY HEAD AND SHOULDERS, I SUPPOSE, OR JUST A FACE SHOT --
REALLY UP TO YOU; PLAY IT BY EAR. HE'S STARING AT US. POSSIBLY YOU
MIGHT WANT TO DRAW A BASIC IMAGE, THEN OVERLAY IT WITH WHITE
DOTTED ZIP-A-TONE.

No dialogue.

Page 24 panel 3

OKAY -- SIMILAR SHOT TO THE FIRST, ONLY WE'RE CLOSE UP ON RIC'S FACE.
AND FELIX'S FACE COMES IN AT ONE SIDE, IN CLOSE-UP, TALKING TO HIM. RIC
IS REALLY QUITE BLANK -- HE HAS NO IDEAS LEFT, AND NEVER WILL HAVE.
HE'S STILL SMART, BUT HE'LL NEVER HAVE ANOTHER ORIGINAL THOUGHT
AGAIN IN HIS LIFE. HE ISN'T REGISTERING ANYTHING THAT FELIX IS SAYING.

Felix:There was no-one there. In the room. There was just a book.

Ric:I don't know... It doesn't connect with anything... It's a name...

Ric:I wish I could remember...

Page 24 panel 4

SAME AS PANEL 2, ALTHOUGH IF YOU WANT TO BE FANCY YOU COULD MAKE IT
A DIFFERENT SHOT, I SUPPOSE, BUT IT'S NOW A SMALLER IMAGE OF THE
SANDMAN STARING AT US. WHITE PANEL. BASICALLY WE'RE LOOKING AT RIC'S
MIND HERE.

No dialogue.

page 24 panel 5

EXTREME CLOSE UP ON RIC. HE LOOKS REALLY BLANK. POSSIBLY RAISED ONE
MESSED-UP FINGER TO HIS LIPS.

Ric:It's so hard to think...

...Morpheus? ...Orpheus? ...One of those...

Page 24 panel 6

SAME AS PANELS 2 AND 4, ONLY THE SANDMAN FIGURE IS TINY NOW.

no dialogue.

Page 24 panel 7

PULL BACK A BIT -- FELIX IS HOLDING OUT THE BOOK TO RIC, WHO'S STILL
SITTING, SLIGHTLY HUNCHED, STARING INTO SPACE, AND DOESN'T REGISTER
IT.

Felix:You can take it with you to the hospital, Richard.
Ric:She's gone, you see. And it's all gone with her. Everything. All of them, all the
dreams...

Ric:No... I can't remember. I've lost it...

Page 24 panel 8

WHITE PANEL.

No dialogue.

Page 24 panel 9

OKAY -- FINAL SHOT IS OF RIC, LOOKING AT US, UNFOCUSED. TRY TO ECHO --
THOUGH NOT COPY -- THE FIRST SHOT WE SAW, PAGE 1 PANEL 1, AT LEAST IN
TERMS OF THE SIZE OF THE FACE, AND THE DIRECTION IT'S LOOKING. HE
LOOKS HURT, WOUNDED, DESTROYED, MESSED UP. ZOMBIE.

Ric:It's gone.

Ric:I've got no idea any more.

No idea at all.

Then either END or,
NEXT: A Dream of a Thousand Cats -- whichever you think works best.

CAT-EYES

Okay -- that's it; a bit delayed due to power cuts, caused by hurricane winds
(remember the last time that happened, Karen?) --anyway, if anyone has a
question, ring me. Hope you all like it; enjoy.
best

n.

Dedication:

Four stories for four
good people:
CLIVE BARKER
JILL KARLA SCHWARTZ,
AIMEE HORSTING, and
MIKAL GILMORE.

Hi guys.
Neil.

For **Mom**, who rationalized my
early, odd drawings as normal;
for **Dad**, who watched FRANKENSTEIN
and KOLCHAK, THE NIGHT STALKER with
me; for **Jeff**, who let his little
brother be his friend, as well as
Lynn, Bill, Ed, Steve and **Carol;**
also Robert Pickman, the best
artist ever, Roger Corman, James
Whale, Boris Karloff and Peter
Cushing; and Gustav Quadrangle
for endless inspiration; and finally,
Knuckles, the very patient and
orange model of the "Sandcat".
Kelley.

This one's for "Mr. Sandman" himself,
Michael Wm Kaluta, who taught me
a lot about making dreams come true.
Charles.

For my mother and father.
Colleen

To Inell Jones.
Malcolm